The Democratic Party

Dr. Peter J. Ling

The Democratic Party

A Photographic History

THUNDER BAY
P·R·E·S·S

San Diego, California

Thunder Bay Press
An imprint of the Advantage Publishers Group
5880 Oberlin Drive, San Diego, CA 92121-4794
www.thunderbaybooks.com

All notations of errors or omissions should be addressed to Thunder Bay Press, Editorial
Department, at the above address. All other correspondence (author inquiries, permissions)
concerning the content of this book should be addressed to Getty Images, 21–31 Woodfield Road,
London W9 2BA, England.

ISBN 1-59223-063-6
Library of Congress Cataloging-in-Publication Data available upon request.

Printed in Singapore
1 2 3 4 5 07 06 05 04 03

Editor: Edward Horton
Design: Tea McAleer
Picture Research: Jennifer Jeffrey
Production: Mary Osborne
Special thanks: Liz Ihre, Nick Yapp, Franziska Payer Crockett, Paul Welti, Ali Khoja

Page 1

President Lyndon B. Johnson and Vice President
Hubert Humphrey on LBJ Ranch in 1964, the
high point of their administration.

Pages 2–3

President Franklin D. Roosevelt at his Hyde
Park estate in 1939, in a characteristically
upbeat mood—and with his trademark
prop, a cigarette holder.

Contents

Introduction 7

Chapter One
Growing Pains 14
1824–1860

Chapter Two
Fighting Back 42
1861–1896

Chapter Three
The Wilson Interlude 84
1896–1932

Chapter Four
The New Deal 138
1933–1941

Chapter Five
World War and Cold War 196
1941–1960

Chapter Six
Broken Dreams 250
1960–1980

Chapter Seven
A New Kind of Democrat 314
1981–2003

Editor's Note 363

Picture Acknowledgments 364

Index 366

Foreword from the Chairman of the Democratic National Committee

THE HISTORY OF the Democratic Party is the history of the United States. Founded by Thomas Jefferson, the Democratic Party is the oldest political party in the world, and Jefferson's vision of a Republic based on Liberty and Equality has remained a driving vision of America and the Democratic Party.

The imprint of the Democratic Party is ever evident throughout America's history. When women were denied the vote it was President Wilson's vision to get the Nineteenth Amendment to expand the suffrage to include women. When America's economy faltered and there was a profound economic and political crisis, it was Franklin Delano Roosevelt's optimism and creativity that saw America through the dark days of the Great Depression. When the world was threatened by dictators bent on conquest, it was FDR and then Harry Truman who defeated one set of dictators and stopped the expansion of Communism.

And when America finally confronted its ugliest stain, racism and bigotry, it was Lyndon Johnson who helped right profound wrongs with a whirlwind of legislative accomplishments that put the federal government on the side of civil rights for all Americans. The two great hallmarks of lifting senior citizens from poverty, Social Security and Medicare, were born of the Democratic Party's concern for America's elderly.

President Jimmy Carter set a high standard for presidential involvement in peace negotiations by successfully negotiating peace between Israel and Egypt, which resulted in the Camp David Peace Accord.

The energy and enthusiasm brought to the White House by President John F. Kennedy were brought back by President Bill Clinton, who led this country into a period of historic economic prosperity. We believe that strong leaders and fresh ideas can improve the lives of every American. The Democratic Party will always believe that we can make the difference in the life of one child, one family, and one nation. We are proud of the legacy our leaders are leaving this world and we are working every day to fulfill their promises of a better tomorrow.

Terry McAuliffe

Perhaps the most popular
Democratic politician never to
reach the White House, Adlai
Stevenson is remembered for his
quick intelligence and for the
grace with which he twice
campaigned against the
unbeatable Ike, in 1952 and
four years later (left).

Introduction

"We used to say that the ideal of government was for every man
to be left alone and not interfered with. That was the idea that
obtained in Jefferson's time. But we are coming now to realize
that life is so complicated that we are not dealing with old
conditions, and that the law has to step in and create new
conditions under which we may live."

Woodrow Wilson (1912)

THE DEMOCRATIC PARTY—the party of Thomas Jefferson and Andrew Jackson, of Woodrow Wilson and FDR, of JFK and Bill Clinton—has been a party of enduring leadership but changing principles. Parodied by recent critics as the party of big government addicted to "tax and spend" policies, Democrats were once the champions of limited government and low taxation. An early Jeffersonian maxim—"Eternal vigilance is the price of liberty"—reflected not just a populist suspicion that those who put on airs and graces are untrustworthy, but the abiding conviction that power corrupts and must therefore be severely curtailed.

Compared to their Whig and later Republican rivals, nineteenth-century Democrats trusted the common people and worried more about the prospect of tyranny being imposed from above than of anarchy breaking out from below. When Jackson refused to grant a new charter to the Bank of the United States in 1832, he saw himself as the people's champion, killing a "monster" and ending "a concentration of power in the hands of a few" that was "dangerous to public liberty."

For Democrats, virtually into the twentieth century, mistrust of the powerful reinforced their devotion to another of Jefferson's sayings—"the government that governs least governs best." The same fear of power's tendency to corrupt made Democrats prefer state and local to national government. After all, keeping politicians honest seemed somewhat more feasible if they were not way off in Washington. The ever-present threat of tyranny similarly ensured that early Democrats liked their definition of the U.S. Constitution to be strict. If the Constitution was unclear about any question—such as the legality of extending slavery to the new Western territories, for example—the Democratic position was to avoid loose constitutional interpretation. The federal government should step aside and let local people decide.

Given this mistrust of government in principle, early Democrats believed in keeping the federal budget balanced. If a surplus arose in the federal Treasury due to the sale of lands or increased revenue from import duties, Democrats wanted Congress to pass the surplus back to the states. Democrats were equally hostile to taxes. This was partly due to the fact that early farm settlers actually had very little hard cash, and taxes were one of the crucial costs that demanded cash. Taxes were still so suspect in Andrew Jackson's time that Democrats argued among themselves over just how abominable the newly approved import tariff actually was. Some denied its value altogether; others pleaded that there was a genuine need for federal revenue. South Carolinians demanded an instant reduction in the tax, threatening secession if none came.

Thomas Jefferson, a Founding Father whose political philosophy underpins both major political parties of the American republic.

Andrew Jackson, the Democrats' adoptive father, fought privilege by vetoing the National Bank charter, yet ironically has been immortalized on the $20 bill.

Franklin Delano Roosevelt made Washington appear a friend to ordinary Americans during the Great Depression of the 1930s.

It was the Whig-Republicans who insisted that the tariff protected American industry and hence the American workingman, but for Democrats, it remained a tax and therefore obnoxious, by definition. "Every cent taken from the people beyond that required for their protection by the government," Grover Cleveland declared in 1884, "is no better than robbery." Eight years later the party platform angrily complained that the Republican tariff was "a robbery of the great majority of the American people for the benefit of the few."

Rich men have always seemed able to get the ear of government, and in reaction, Democrats became traditional defenders of the unheeded common people. "All over this land are the homes of forgotten men," declared Democratic presidential nominee William Jennings Bryan in 1900, "men whose rights are disregarded, men whose interests are neglected because of the demands made by combined capital." In similar fashion, Franklin Roosevelt described his New Deal as a program for "the forgotten man." True, some New Dealers had an enormous faith in the benevolent power of the state, but FDR's position that federal power should grow only so far as to enable government to protect the individual from private corporate power stated Democratic core values. "No business is above government," he vowed in 1940, "and government must be empowered to deal adequately with any business that tries to rise above government."

Jefferson's suspicion of power and privilege bequeathed to latter-day Democrats a suspicion of entrenched elites. Such antagonism partly explains the party's abiding appeal to the poor farmer and the new immigrant, both groups likely to be looked down on and even despised by the Whig-Republicans as not worthy of a civic role. According to historian Richard Hofstader, political revolt in America has tended to be "against monopolies and special privileges in both the economic and the political spheres, against social distinctions and the restriction of credit, [and] against limits upon the avenues of personal advancements." As the antithesis to Whig-Republicanism, the Democratic Party has proved the logical home for the rebellious and the disaffected.

Not every rebellion, however, is for a good cause. In defense of Southern slavery, the rebellious tendency led the party into secession and civil war in 1860–61. And for generations thereafter, resentment of moral lectures from the well-to-do on a host of moral topics from temperance to the treatment of convicts reinforced the prejudices of the common folk. The South was solidly Democratic after the Civil War and by the century's end increasingly segregationist. But ultimately, the Democrats' enduring egalitarian impulse in the decades after World War II finally overturned white supremacy.

The shift was signaled in 1948. President Harry Truman's basic appeal in that year remained one of New Deal–style egalitarianism. In a barnstorming tour of the nation, "Give 'em Hell" Harry celebrated the Democratic Party as "the people's party" and decried the Republicans as "the party of special interest." "The Republicans' rich man's tax bill," he roared, "sticks a knife into the back of the poor." But to the consternation of white Southern Dixiecrats who bolted the party as a consequence, the national Democratic Party finally made an explicit bid for African American votes in 1948. In consequence, the idea of federal protection of rights as being the necessary safeguard for fairness and equality in subsequent decades took on very distinctive social and cultural connotations, which came increasingly to define the Democratic Party in contrast to the Republican Party.

It was a change to the Democrats' character that caused dismay among many traditional Southern and Northern white working-class supporters. A continuing emphasis to the present day on rights and toleration has allowed the Republican Party to corner the "law and order" issue to a large extent. "New Democrats" of the Clinton era have had to prove that they are tough on crime and hardheaded on welfare. The national Democratic Party worried social conservatives when it affirmed "the right to be different" in 1972, and the 1984 Democratic Convention increased these anxieties when it resolved that, "Government has a special responsibility to those whom society has historically prevented from enjoying the benefits of full citizenship for reasons of race, religion, sex, age, national origin and ethnic heritage, sexual orientation, or disability." Declaring itself "the party of inclusion" in 1992, the party took "special pride" in America's "emergence as the world's largest and most successful multiethnic, multiracial republic." At local level this inclusiveness has kept the party competitive with the Republicans, but in the race for the White House in particular, liberal tolerance has been a less successful platform for the party since 1968.

In the 1990s political pundits were apt to explain Democratic electoral misfortunes in part by referring to "angry white males." Certainly, when Thomas Jefferson penned the immortal words "All men are created equal" for the Declaration of Independence in 1776, he did not have anyone in mind other than white males. Two centuries had to pass before most Southern politicians abandoned hostility to the idea of

New Deal programs like the TVA epitomized Democratic faith in federal power for public good, providing cheap electricity and ensuring the nation's defense.

Against the odds and Republican dirty tricks, "Give 'em Hell" Harry Truman won the presidency in 1948. His winning strategy was to attack Republican privilege and greed and to support civil rights.

political and social equality for African Americans. The Democratic Party's reverence for rights has been the logical fulfillment of their interpretation of the core of the American Creed. Democrats have peppered their recent rhetoric with references to "human rights." The Clinton-style New Democrat was renowned for having far more sensitivity toward minority concerns than was to be found in the Republican Party of Pat Buchanan. Despite expressing a willingness to accept welfare reform to nurture personal responsibility, Democrats on the whole remained more likely to urge the retention of human welfare programs in the face of Republican calls for even bigger tax breaks.

This tendency to appeal to morality rather than economic advantage has been a feature of twentieth-century Democratic foreign policy as well. Woodrow Wilson's attempt to link American intervention in World War I to moral principles and to the establishment of an international forum to ensure mutual security and advance moral aims, set the stage for this long-standing Democratic internationalism. Accepting the immense challenge of World War II, Roosevelt and Truman defined American policy in idealistic terms of freedom and proceeded to develop international institutions such as the United Nations to advance moral principles. From Berlin to Kosovo, Kennedy, Johnson, Carter, and Clinton all sought to couch their foreign policy goals in moral terms.

The Vietnam War was an exercise in moral policing that went seriously wrong, but while this clearly weakened the interventionist impulse, it did not end Democratic internationalism. It merely strengthened contradictory factions within the party—radicals who charged that U.S. foreign policy needed to be recast on moral lines and conservatives interested in a pragmatic formulation of policy primarily through Congress—around the common conviction that presidents should not be given unlimited discretion over foreign policy.

When Republicans have held the White House in recent years, Democrats have criticized the GOP's apparent indifference to morality—as witness Reagan's illicit arms sales to Iran and his covert backing of the Contras in Nicaragua. They have also deplored Republican unilateralism, most recently during the buildup to the war against Iraq. During the Clinton administration, however, Democratic divisions slowed the emergence of a vigorous and consistent foreign policy, thereby prolonging the period of selective engagement in the international arena that George H. W. Bush began. This has become a prelude for George W. Bush's "go-it-alone" philosophy.

Marching through the Deep South for voters' rights, Dr. Martin Luther King Jr. transformed the Democratic Party into a multicultural coalition.

To capture the character of the Democratic Party, one must consider not just its evolving principles and policies, but people. Yeoman farmers pursuing their dream of agricultural prosperity and workingmen striving to own their own workshops were the essential Democratic figures of the nineteenth century. The rural poor and the wage-earning urban union man became the party's mainstays in the 1930s. Since the 1960s the educated career woman, the African American, and the gay or environmental activist have all been Democratic stereotypes. Campaign managers—desperately eager to avoid yet another long period of Republican dominance—have recently tried to puncture such stereotypes, while at the same time ensuring that the party does indeed retain most of the votes of women, African Americans, and liberal activists of whatever individual concern. Ultimately, however, the political professionals have felt that the wider public as represented in their focus groups will embrace the politics of the "Rainbow Coalition" only if Democratic policies look and sound basically mainstream and white. Such apparent contradictions are not easily resolved.

Parties have always been coalitions and diversity is usually essential to their success. For most of the Democratic Party's long history, this fact was borne out by the party's success as an alliance of the cotton-growing South and the immigrant city. Both parts of this coalition were shrewd exponents of political leverage. Sectional unity made the South a disproportionate force in national party deliberations until 1936, the first national convention not to require the Democratic presidential nominee to win two thirds of the delegates. Democrats are aware that since 1964 only Southerners have been successful presidential standard-bearers for their party. The Democratic Leadership Council has recognized that although Southern Democratic support is the key to success, the primary schedule favors Northern liberals.

At the local level, metropolitan politics has usually rewarded the bloc vote. A by-product of the world's first mass electorate, the Democratic Party pioneered the "get out the vote" campaign. At its worst, this bred corrupt machine politics of the "Boss Tweed" variety, in which voters chose the party ticket and elected "bosses" in return for favors of various kinds. New York's Tammany Hall and similar bodies in other cities became enduring institutions that reformers struggled to demolish. Ordinary voters felt that these institutions had a very direct interest in their lives. At its best, the quest for mass support provided Democrats with active lines of communication from the local ward to the national convention and placed politics at the vibrant heart of the nation.

FDR persuaded millions of Americans that good government meant active government—and gave them the confidence to work a way through the Great Depression.

Smooth sailing: The young Jack and Jackie Kennedy exuded style in a way no other White House occupants have matched.

For Bill Clinton, leadership meant welfare reform and deficit reduction to preserve vital achievements like Social Security from Republican attacks.

Nothing galvanizes followers or energizes parties like leadership, and this volume offers a roster from the Democratic hall of fame. Even if we allow the Republicans a small claim to Jefferson, it is an imposing list. Franklin Roosevelt—America's only four-time presidential victor— stands at its head, although for many Americans, John F. Kennedy also remains in a class of his own. Equally striking are the Democratic First Ladies. In a bygone age, Frances Cleveland was considered one of the great beauties of the age. From Eleanor Roosevelt to Jackie Kennedy and Hillary Clinton, the Democratic Party can claim that its First Ladies had more political or cultural clout than such Republican counterparts as Mamie Eisenhower, Pat Nixon, or Nancy Reagan. Democrats have even selected more interesting losers. In defeat, William Jennings Bryan and Adlai Stevenson command historical recognition in a way that Republicans like Charles Evans Hughes and Alfred M. Landon do not.

To tell the history of the Democratic Party is inevitably also to tell much of the history of the nation. Democrats were not its only pioneers, of course, but their support of westward expansion as the nation's Manifest Destiny was crucial to America's westward migration. Americans, not just Democrats, responded to the nation's call to arms from the Spanish- American War of 1898 through the two world wars and other foreign conflicts of the last century. By fighting in 1898, however, Southern Democrats underlined their restored place in the Union. Equally significant in the case of both world wars, the party occupied the White House and was prepared to advance U.S. foreign policy by force of arms. With the exceptions of recent Republican presidents (Reagan and the Bushes), it has tended to be Democrats who have called upon the nation's sons to die for freedom.

All history is prologue. Today's Democratic Party must wrestle with many of the problems that beset its forefathers. There is a mistrust of government among many Americans comparable to that felt by early Democrats, and in many quarters there is a call for low taxes and a reduced federal government. But at the same time there is a recognition that Woodrow Wilson remains right. No matter how much we wish to be just left alone to get on with our lives, the world is so complex and dangerous that we need government to help us deal with its complexity, alleviate our fears, and ensure our security. If the Democratic Party can find leaders to meet these needs, it will enjoy renewed success. The ideals of the party remain true and inspiring, and the opportunity to rebuild a winning coalition may be just an economic downturn away.

Chapter One
Growing Pains
1824–1860

Growing Pains
1824–1860

THE ANCESTRAL GHOSTS OF THE DEMOCRATIC PARTY must have watched the 2000 election with an eerie sense that they had seen all this before. There was their beloved party's nominee, Al Gore, a distinguished political son of Tennessee, fighting for the White House against George W. Bush, the son of a former Republican president. In terms of the popular vote, Gore was the victor, but after weeks of controversy that made "chad" into a political buzzword, the election was awarded to Bush. It sounded like 1824 all over again, when the defeat of the rough and ready Indian fighter from Tennessee, Andrew Jackson, effectively launched the Democratic Party.

In a four-way contest, Jackson won a majority of the popular vote, but did not get a majority in the electoral college. The choice of president therefore fell to the House of Representatives. The House, encouraged by its speaker Henry Clay, chose John Q. Adams, the son of former president John Adams. Clay was swiftly appointed secretary of state, the traditional staging post for the presidency in those days. Fighting the "corrupt bargain" between Adams and Clay in 1828 prompted Jacksonian Democrats to develop the first real national party network. Their efforts coincided with legal changes that extended the right to vote to most adult white males—a rarity in the world. Local groups sponsored parades, barbecues, and other popular events to attract the growing electorate to both Jackson and a slate of local candidates.

Jackson's opponents tried to belittle him as an ignorant frontier ruffian or potential military despot. He had proved insubordinate to civilian authority when he raided Spanish Florida in 1816, and he had waged war on the Seminole Indians two years later without congressional authority. When critics also uncovered the fact that Mrs. Jackson was technically still married to her first husband, Democrats rallied to their leader, whom they nicknamed "Old Hickory." To this day, the jackass, or donkey, chosen by Jackson's enemies to symbolize his ignorance, is the symbol of the Democratic Party.

Of course, the Democrats gave as good as they got in this mudslinging battle. John Quincy Adams's past career as a diplomat in Europe and his somewhat haughty demeanor provided ammunition.

An 1830s cartoon depicts Andrew Jackson as a jackass. It mocks his loyal followers, but Democrats proudly made the donkey symbol their own.

Previous pages: Heading west, Americans quarreled over how the land should be developed. Should it be free soil or equally open to Southerners and their slaves? It was a question that divided parties and ultimately the nation.

"**King Andrew**," his enemies cried, when Jackson used the presidential veto more than any previous president. Jobs and favors for loyalty further fanned the flames.

"**Old Hickory**" photographed shortly before his death in 1848 at the age of seventy-eight.

According to Democratic publicists, as U.S. minister to Russia the decadent Adams had courted favor with the czar by supplying him with a string of willing girls. He had subsequently taken his other vices into the White House, which he had fitted out with "gambling equipment"—a somewhat lavish description for a chess set and a billiard table.

The Jacksonians' main policy thrust was to rid government of class bias. They defended rotation in office rather than unlimited tenure to prevent the entrenchment of elites, although enemies retorted that mass appointments after each election created a "spoils system." As Vice President Martin Van Buren's successful network for party operations in New York, the "Albany Regency" had demonstrated, patronage was a vital tool of party management. In the early republic, government activity was very limited by today's standards, with official business at the state level only taking up a few weeks a year, but there were still gains to be made from it. Jackson's rivals, for instance, favored renewing the charter of the Second Bank of the United States to regulate credit. Since the national bank held federal deposits, its credit was assured, and its privileged shareholders, such as the bank's president, Nicholas Biddle, could offer loans to elite associates, while denying credit to others.

Vetoing the bank's new charter because it gave a handful of unelected, wealthy individuals control over the credit levers of the national economy, Jackson portrayed himself as the champion of the common man. But his subsequent removal of government deposits to twenty-three "pet" state banks smacked of still more patronage. The legacy of Jackson was to present the Democrats as being for simple local government. It was his adversaries, the forebears of the Republicans (the Whigs), who wanted more governmental intervention, whether in the form of federal backing for roads and canals or prescriptive social legislation against alcohol, gambling (presumably excluding chess and billiards), and unrestricted immigration.

A coalition of Southern rural and Northeastern urban voters, the Democratic Party before the Civil War was a potent electoral force in the world's first mass democracy. Between 1828 and 1860, six out of nine presidential elections went its way. The ability of the party to get out the vote was even begrudgingly acknowledged by its rivals. Whigs complained that Democrats unthinkingly "worshiped at the shrine of the party." The hint of anti-Catholicism in the "shrine" reference reflected the Democrats' embrace of immigrant Americans, especially the Irish, whom their opponents openly despised. Irish immigration grew steadily in the Jackson era, and then soared with the exodus from the catastrophic potato famine in the late 1840s. Young, poor, unskilled, and often non-English speaking, the Irish banded together for self-defense and mutual aid and formed an important political bloc. The Democrats remained the natural party for new Americans.

The popularity of Democrats in the South was hugely significant for the slavery question. Even when slavery was not directly involved, the sectional divide was hard to bridge. The 1828 tariff, raised to protect New England and Western economic interests, was fiercely resented in the South. In a famous congressional debate, South Carolina's Robert Hayne warned Massachusetts Whig Daniel Webster that individual states would use their sovereignty to nullify federal laws that damaged their interests. As the nullification crisis grew, despite being both a Southerner and a slaveholder, Jackson made a stand for federal power and implied that he would use force to preserve the union. A reduction in the tariff, however, helped to defuse the situation.

The sectional split always threatened party unity. As antislavery agitation grew in the 1830s, some Southern Democrats, notably Senator John C. Calhoun of South Carolina, proved fiery defenders of their region's "peculiar institution." They flatly refused to consider antislavery petitions in Congress. This deepened the impression that slavery threatened the republic's civil liberties. Other Southern Democrats, such as James Polk of Tennessee (who in 1844 became America's youngest president to date, aged forty-nine), used patriotism to unite Americans and urged westward expansion to fulfill the nation's Manifest Destiny.

Land hunger had previously fed the harsh Indian removal policy of the Jackson era. Native Americans still held immense areas of the South and West when Jackson took office in 1829. The Black Hawk War of 1832 was sparked by white seizure of Native American lands in Illinois. Captured, the dignified Black Hawk won sympathy, which cost nothing, but not justice. So-called civilized tribes such as the Cherokee in Georgia had adapted to the new economy, even holding black slaves for plantation work, but this did not make their presence acceptable. Congress passed the Indian Removal Act in 1830, which established a policy of forcible removal of tribes from their lands to the Oklahoma territory. Cherokee removal was the most prolonged. It culminated in the "Trail of Tears" in 1836, a forced march during which 4,000 of the 15,000 Native Americans died en route. Threat of removal triggered the Second Seminole War in Florida in 1835, which dragged on until 1842.

During his military career Jackson had fought the Seminole in Florida in 1817–18, and during his presidency they rose up again to resist white incursions in 1835 (illustration above).

Black Hawk became a celebrity when he was sent back east in 1833. His dignity made some question Jackson's policy of pacification and removal, but land hunger ruled.

Territorial expansion was urged as a means of sustaining the American Dream of land ownership, but congressional battles over the annexation of Texas in 1845 and the Mexican War of 1846–48 showed that the issue was inseparable from slavery. Texans had won their own independence in 1836 through the heroics of men like Davy Crockett at the Alamo and the military leadership of Sam Houston. But the vast Lone Star Republic might reasonably be annexed not as one, but several slave states, and this slowed its admission. Northern Democrats' hostility to the admission of new slave states threatened a party split. Congressman David Wilmot of Pennsylvania introduced a resolution in 1846 forbidding the establishment of slavery in any acquired Mexican territory, and former president Martin Van Buren championed the exclusion of slavery from the West as the unsuccessful candidate of the breakaway Free-Soil Party in 1848. Such figures tried to reinforce the sanctity of the so-called Missouri Compromise, which had resolved an earlier conflict over the expansion of slavery in 1820 by agreeing that slavery was forever prohibited in any unorganized territory north of Missouri's southern boundary.

Battle of Monterey, 1846. Polk's Manifest Destiny policy brought triumphant war with Mexico, but it also added to deepening internal American divisions.

Compared to rival Whigs, the Democrats hung together better as sectional tensions deepened in the 1850s. Despite straddling the Missouri Compromise line that had determined a territory's slave or free status since 1820, California was admitted as a free state by the Compromise of 1850. It was simply too valuable to be allowed to stay outside the Union. Its admission produced a free state majority in the Senate, which Southerners reluctantly conceded in return for a tough new Fugitive Slave Law. Attacking the new law as a crime against humanity, Harriet Beecher Stowe's dramatic novel *Uncle Tom's Cabin*, with its noble slaves and evil slave catchers, became an instant best-seller after serialization in 1852. It suggested that men like Daniel Webster who had compromised with slavery to preserve the Union were complicit in the corruption that slavery inevitably involved. Predictably, the book outraged the South by its moving celebration of African American piety and portrayal of white Southern depravity. The Compromise of 1850 effectively destroyed the Whigs, but Democrats still clung to the possibility of sectional reconciliation. The Democratic nominee in 1852, Mexican War hero Franklin Pierce of New Hampshire, was determined to unite the party by being a "Northern man with Southern principles." With the catchy slogan, "We Polked you in 1844, we shall Pierce you in 1852," the Democrats trounced their Whig rivals for the last time.

San Francisco harbor in the 1850s. Following the discovery of gold in California in 1848, Americans—along with fortune-seekers from all over the world—flooded into the once Mexican province and sped California's admission to the Union.

In choosing Pierce, a relative nonentity, Democrats had spurned the leadership potential of the "Little Giant," Senator Stephen Douglas of Illinois. Just five feet four inches tall, Douglas was a heavy-drinking bundle of energy and eloquence who believed that he could resolve the question of slavery in the territories through the doctrine of "popular sovereignty." In true Democratic style, this held that the local people, rather than Congress, should decide whether or not to permit slavery in a territory or state. Douglas secured passage of the Kansas-Nebraska Act in 1854, which applied the popular sovereignty principle and confirmed the abandonment of the Missouri Compromise line.

Unfortunately for Douglas, what followed in Kansas was not a neat solution by popular vote, but a mini civil war. Following Northern attempts to encourage the migration of antislavery settlers to Kansas prior to territorial elections in 1855, proslavery "Border Ruffians" from Missouri swept in, pledging to kill every "God-damned abolitionist in the Territory." By 1856 rival governments vied for recognition, and both sides were engaged in a vicious guerilla war. The violence even spilled onto the floor of the Senate. Outraged by insults to his region, state, and family, Democratic congressman Preston Brooks of South Carolina smashed abolitionist Senator Charles Sumner of Massachusetts over the head with his ebony cane, just yards from where Douglas sat. Censured, Brooks resigned, only to be triumphantly reelected by his Carolinian constituents who showered him with new canes.

"Bleeding Sumner" and "Bleeding Kansas" ensured that Douglas was too great a liability to be Democratic nominee in 1856. Instead, the party chose a veteran politician, James Buchanan of Pennsylvania, who had already courted Southern support by his calls for the annexation of Cuba. With a majority of Southern states and five free states, Buchanan had a comfortable majority in the electoral college, but ominously his divided opponents—the new Republican Party and a third party, the American, or "Know-Nothing," Party—gained more popular votes because of their Northern appeal.

By this stage, a generation of Democratic Party dominance had left its mark on the U.S. Supreme Court, with most of the justices being Southerners who owed their nomination to Democratic presidents from Jackson onward. Consequently, in 1857, when Chief Justice Roger Taney issued a sweeping opinion in the *Dred Scott v. Sanford* case, his judgment was seen in highly partisan terms. Scott was a slave who sued for his freedom on the grounds that he had resided with his master for several years in free territory. According to Taney, not only had Scott remained a

FORCING SLAVERY DOWN THE THROAT OF A FRE

Free-soilers included Northern Democrats who complained that to woo Southern support, party leaders like Stephen Douglas and James Buchanan had forced the prospect of blacks in the West down their throats.

"Little Giant" Stephen Douglas of Illinois tried to end the debate over slavery in the territories: The local people should decide, he argued. In the end, his 1854 Kansas-Nebraska Act led to war.

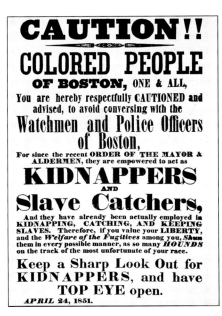

New England abolitionists resisted the Fugitive Slave Act of 1850 and organized to prevent the return of alleged slaves. Southern Democrats reacted with outrage.

Dred Scott was a slave who sued for freedom on the grounds that he had lived in free territory. His appeal to the U.S. Supreme Court in 1857 was comprehensively rejected.

slave, despite his sojourn in free territory, but any attempt by Congress to exclude slavery anywhere was an unconstitutional denial of property rights. Furious antislavery opponents reacted by claiming that the whole past decade of Democratic rule was actually a successful "Slave Power" conspiracy in which the annexation of Texas, the Mexican War, and the repudiation of the Missouri Compromise had all happened due to the plotting of powerful Southern slaveholders.

Buchanan's endorsement of a proslavery constitution in Kansas in 1858 deepened this impression of Southern bias and forced Northern Democrats like Douglas to reexamine their own position in the upcoming elections. Breaking with Buchanan over the proposed Kansas constitution, Douglas entered his Senate reelection battle against a relatively unknown Republican opponent, Abraham Lincoln, determined to defend his policy of popular sovereignty. In a series of public debates, he and Lincoln argued over the implications of the Dred Scott decision. When Douglas insisted that local people in any state or territory could effectively exclude slavery simply by refusing to pass a legal code to protect it, Lincoln countered that the Union would not endure, half-slave and half-free. It would inevitably become either wholly slave or wholly free. Posterity remembers Lincoln's words, but the voters chose Douglas.

Held in Charleston, South Carolina, the 1860 Democratic Convention saw Southern proslavery zealots, or "firebrands," attempt to force into the party platform demands for a federal slave code to operate in the territories. When these proslavery planks were voted down, the majority of Southern delegates walked out. Reconvening in the less hostile atmosphere of Baltimore, Northern Democrats ditched Buchanan and nominated Douglas for president. Almost simultaneously Southern Democrats met separately to name Vice President John Breckinridge of Kentucky as their presidential candidate. This sectional split virtually ensured a Republican victory, which the Southern firebrands warned would equally certainly mean secession. Worn down by excessive drinking and ill health that would see him dead within a year, Douglas pleaded for Southern support for the Union, but he ran behind Breckinridge and the Constitutional Union Party candidate John Bell in the South. His tally of 1,376,957 votes was bettered by Lincoln, who, even with no Southern support, polled around 400,000 more. The White House was in Republican hands, but the clear majority who voted for either Douglas or Breckinridge showed that the Democratic Party retained local support that would ensure its recovery once the sectional crisis had been settled by war rather than politics.

THE BATTLE OF NEW ORLEANS, FOUGHT JAN 8TH 1814.

War Hero Turned Politician

Routing the British at New Orleans in 1815 (above) catapulted Andrew Jackson to national fame. A skilled horseman and noted Indian fighter, Jackson polarized opinion between Democratic followers and his Whig critics. He benefited from a broader franchise and also more sophisticated party management that encouraged local candidates to capitalize on his celebrity (right).

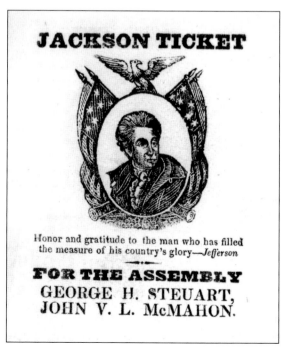

JACKSON TICKET

Honor and gratitude to the man who has filled the measure of his country's glory—*Jefferson*

FOR THE ASSEMBLY
GEORGE H. STEUART,
JOHN V. L. McMAHON.

"Old Hickory"

Jackson could be sympathetically portrayed as a dignified statesman hewn from presidential timber (left). His defeated rivals, however, saw the new mass electorate that chose Jackson as a rabble, especially after they poured into the White House on Inauguration Day (above), causing extensive damage.

UNCLE SAM'S PET PUPS!
Or, Mother BANK'S last refuge.
Sold at ELTON'S, 18 Division-Street, New-York.

The Bank War

The Bank War helped to define the two parties—Democrat and Whig—in the 1830s as part of a larger debate over the role of the federal government in supporting economic activity. Whigs, satirized as trying to provide a refuge for "Mother Bank" (above), had policies to promote industrial development. Democrats preferred to support "pet" state banks. Similar charges of crude favoritism were leveled at Jackson's inner circle or "Kitchen Cabinet," depicted (left) as a cart of government drawn by an ass with Jackson's head. The inclusion of a black man emptying his bucket from a nearby privy into the cart suggests the level of partisan feeling by the mid-1830s.

Currency Crisis

Refusing to renew the charter of the Bank of the United States (above), Andrew Jackson argued that the bank was a tool for the rich against the common man. He would drive these speculators out and destroy their temple. Unfortunately, without the bank to provide monetary stability, states issued their own notes, and the speculation Jackson dreaded, occurred. During the 1837 panic, New York banks refused to redeem notes for hard currency, and critics used mock currency (right) to parody the Democrats' financial mismanagement.

Van Buren's Machine

Jackson's successor, Martin Van Buren (opposite), was a wily New York political operator whose single term (1837–41) was dominated by financial crisis. He ran again for the presidency as the Free-Soil candidate in 1848, as sectional divisions grew. "Little Van" embodied the New York wing of the Democratic Party that came to be associated with Tammany Hall (above), a fraternal organization that delivered the Irish immigrant bloc vote on election day in return for favors of various kinds. Jacksonian Democrats, labeled "Tories" in this woodcut (right), extended their "experiment" to the federal level. The "spoils system" rewarded local party members with political appointments as customhouse officers or postmasters.

Manifest Destiny and Mexico

President James K. Polk (above) was known as "Young Hickory," since he resembled his Tennessee compatriot, Andrew Jackson. Polk entered the White House in 1845, having won popular approval for an aggressive westward expansion policy to achieve America's Manifest Destiny of controlling the entire continent. He nearly provoked war with Britain over the Oregon border and actually did so with Mexico, whose dictatorial leader, General Antonio L. de Santa Anna (right), had already lost the province of Texas to proslavery American settlers in 1836. After eight years of independence under its president Sam Houston (above right), the Republic of Texas was accepted into the Union in December 1844. Its disputed western border with Mexico gave Polk the chance to incite a war to acquire still further territory.

From Heroic Defeat to Victory

"Remember the Alamo," the Texan battle cry of 1836, recalled the fallen heroes killed by Santa Anna's forces at the Alamo mission in San Antonio earlier that year. Among the slain was fabled frontiersman Davy Crockett (above), who had fought with Jackson against the Creek Indians, but switched to his Whig opponents after 1832. His iconic status, yet equivocal politics, suggests how territorial expansion did not automatically strengthen Democrats. The Mexican War that erupted in 1846 provided fresh heroes, such as "Old Rough and Ready," General Zachary Taylor, the victor at Monterey (left), who won the 1848 election for the Whigs. But then, Taylor was also a Southern Whig who brought fifteen of his house slaves to the White House. Democrats could trust such a president. Unfortunately, after celebrating Independence Day 1850 with an excess of cherries and iced milk, Taylor lay dead, leaving the less trusted Millard Fillmore of New York to appease Democrats over slavery.

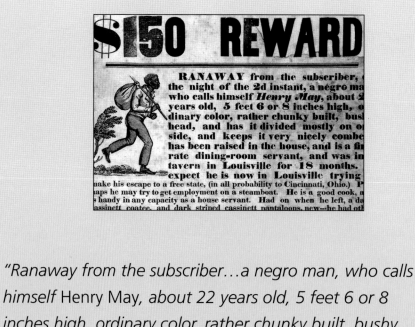

"*Ranaway from the subscriber…a negro man, who calls himself* Henry May, *about 22 years old, 5 feet 6 or 8 inches high, ordinary color, rather chunky built, bushy head, and has it divided mostly on one side, and keeps it very nicely combed; has been raised in the house, and is a first rate dining-room servant…."*

"*Ranaway from the subscriber….The man is a black negro, full height, very erect, his face a little thin. He is about forty years of age, and calls himself* Washington Reed. *He is probably well dressed, possibly takes with him an ivory headed cane, and is of good address. Several of his teeth are gone…."*

The Compromise of 1850

Slaveholders had always fretted over the fact that their prized property had legs and a liking for freedom. Since colonial times, they had advertised for the return of runaways—and expected the authorities to aid them (left). By 1850 Southern planters knew that abolitionists were assisting fugitive slaves. They demanded a law that underlined the obligation of all states to return escaped slaves and gave officials a clear cash incentive to do so. The need to admit gold-rich California quickly to resolve the fate of other territory acquired from Mexico and to calm abolitionist agitation over the shoddy spectacle of slave trading in the nation's capital set the stage for a great debate. To a rapt chamber (above), three elder statesmen—John Calhoun (long-haired on the far right), Henry Clay (speaking), and Daniel Webster (seated, head in hand)—urged compromise to save the Union. Secession loomed otherwise, warned Calhoun, a staunch South Carolinian defender of slavery. Famed for securing the Missouri Compromise of 1820 that had supposedly set a northern limit to slavery's expansion, Clay of Kentucky pleaded for unity three decades later. Bravest politically was Webster of Massachusetts, who knew that not pressing antislavery demands would draw shrill denunciations back home. Eventually the compromise passed. California entered the Union as a free state. New Mexico and Utah became territories. The slave trade ended in the District of Columbia, and the tough Fugitive Slave Law passed. Exhausted politicians concluded that it was the duty of every patriot to get drunk. Virtually the entire Congress obeyed.

Antislavery Propaganda

Since the time of Jackson, abolitionists had been seen as dangerous troublemakers fomenting sectional discord and even slave revolt. Newspaper editor Elijah Lovejoy in Alton, Illinois, had died defending his office (below left) from an antiabolitionist mob in 1837. Had novelist Harriet Beecher Stowe (right) lived outside the abolitionist heartland of New England when she serialized her powerful best-seller *Uncle Tom's Cabin* (left) in 1851–52, Southern zealots might readily have delivered her a similar fate. Her sentimental tale slammed the new Fugitive Slave Law as immoral. According to legend, when Abraham Lincoln met Harriet Beecher Stowe in 1862 he said, "So you're the little woman who wrote the book that started this great war!"

A Demand for Freedom

For many Southern defenders of slavery, slave rebellion was their greatest fear. They regarded men like Frederick Douglass (above), who escaped slavery in Maryland and devoted himself to full-time abolitionist agitation, in much the same way contemporary Americans regard terrorists. Slavery was a recent memory in some Northern states. New York's last remaining slaves, such as Sojourner Truth (right), were not emancipated until 1827. Described by Douglass as "a strange compound of wit and wisdom, of wild enthusiasm and flint-like common sense," the eloquent and spiritual Sojourner electrified female abolitionists with her speech "Ain't I a Woman?" in 1851. By that time, abolitionists had established the Underground Railroad to help slaves flee the South for British Canada. One of its most daring agents was Harriet Tubman (opposite), who returned to the South repeatedly to guide others to freedom. Like Douglass, she was a close associate of white radical abolitionist John Brown and endorsed his plans to arm a slave insurrection.

"Bleeding Kansas"

By the time James Buchanan (left) became president in 1857, Stephen Douglas's attempt to have the issue of slavery settled by the voters of Kansas and Nebraska had degenerated into a mini civil war. Heavily armed, Southern settlers (below) had poured in from neighboring Missouri determined to establish and defend a slave state. Opposing them, Northern abolitionists funded the migration of free-soilers, and zealots like steel-eyed John Brown (right) moved to Kansas prepared to "redeem this nation in blood." Brown murdered five proslavery settlers at Pottawatomie Creek in May 1856. By year's end the death toll in Kansas from atrocities on both sides was 200 and rising. In 1859 Brown was captured in an attack on the federal armory at Harpers Ferry in West Virginia. Southern fury soared when Brown was eulogized in the North. Julia Ward Howe's stirring "John Brown's Body" was a song few Democrats sang.

California Dreaming

This image of the California gold rush in some respects epitomizes the spirit of America at midcentury. The discovery of gold attracted immigrants and native-born Americans who believed that they had a chance to find a fortune and transform their lives. They expected to do so through their own energy and with very little oversight. They intended to stake a claim and were prepared to fight to defend it, but the practicalities of wrestling wealth, or even a living, from the land usually required collective effort. If they were neither first nor powerful, forty-niners found themselves working for someone else and became ever more conscious of the gulf that separated them from the successful. Panning and washing was hard, dirty work that required men to be well fed and durably clothed. The unshaven men posing for the camera may not have made their own fortunes, but they swelled the bank accounts of enterprising merchants. One such was a German Jewish immigrant who made hard-wearing pants—Levi Strauss.

Whose White House?

By 1860 the two-party system that had held together the nation's rival sections had disintegrated. From the ruins of the Whig Party and Northern Free-Soil Democrats, a new entirely Northern party, the Republicans, had emerged a few years earlier. The Democratic Party continued and offered the best hope of sectional unity, but by 1860 its chief Northern claimant to the White House, Stephen Douglas, was unable to command Southern support, and no Southern candidate, like John Breckinridge, could muster the Northern vote. Divided, the Democrats were counted out by a solid Northern vote for Abraham Lincoln in November 1860. Buchanan, the last Democrat to occupy the White House for nearly a quarter of a century, spent his final winter in the Oval Office deciding he could do nothing to stop the course of secession. As soon as the Republican victory was announced, secessionists in South Carolina, Mississippi, Florida, Alabama, Georgia, Louisiana, and Texas made plans to leave the Union. By February 9, 1861, they had done so. The presidential mansion with its manicured lawn and curving driveway remained open to the public and awaited its new president in the spring of 1861, but its quiet elegance was deceiving. By summer Lincoln would hear gunfire from the White House, as war tried to settle what party politics had so evidently not.

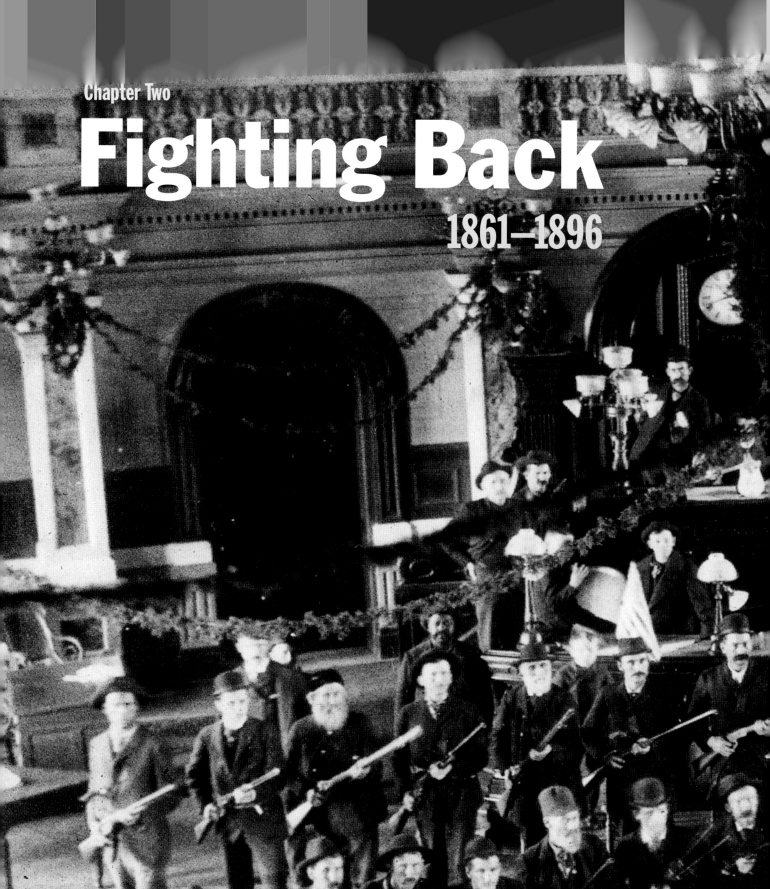

Chapter Two
Fighting Back
1861–1896

Fighting Back
1861–1896

THE ESTABLISHMENT OF A SOUTHERN CONFEDERACY in 1861 was the gravest threat the Democratic Party ever faced. The Southern bloc—the springboard for Democratic national success—departed, and simultaneously every Democrat's loyalty was called into question. Republicans called Northern Democrats "Copperheads," poisonous snakes within the Union. Even after reunion, Republicans insisted that they alone were patriots. The nearly 1.4 million voters who had backed Democratic presidential contender Stephen Douglas in November 1860, nonetheless, did not disappear. In New York and southern portions of the Midwest especially, there was strong Democratic opposition. As open warfare at Fort Sumter in April 1861 was followed by a second wave of secession and then a defeat for the North at the first Battle of Bull Run in July, support for the Democrats rose.

Across the country, men signed up to fight with their friends and neighbors, and governors chose officers for the new military units to cement political bonds. Traditionally Democratic voters, Irish and German immigrants volunteered to fight for the Union to which they had only recently sworn allegiance. While a former Democratic senator, Jefferson Davis, headed the Confederacy, there were leading Democrats on the Union side as well. Secretary of War Edwin Stanton and Tennessee senator Andrew Johnson enabled Lincoln to claim bipartisan support, and after Bull Run, a dashing general, George B. McClellan, took charge of the federal forces. This "Young Napoleon," as McClellan was talked up in the newspapers, was enormously ambitious, politically as well as militarily, and he was a Democrat. McClellan had no time for Lincoln—or "the idiot," as he referred to the president, when he was not calling him "a baboon" or "the original gorilla"—and even less for the idea of abolishing slavery. He wanted "the Constitution as it is, the Union as it was," and as it would turn out he also wanted the presidency in 1864. Unfortunately for Democrats, their "Napoleon" could not win a decisive battle. He did a brilliant job of whipping the Army of the Potomac into shape after the demoralizing defeat at Bull Run, but he then proceeded to baffle everyone—especially his commander in chief— by his reluctance to commit this superb fighting force to battle. Perhaps

At first men flocked to the colors, but as war dragged on into 1863, conscription became necessary. Controversially, the well-off were able to hire substitutes and avoid service.

Previous pages: Even after the Civil War, American politics teetered on the brink of renewed armed conflict. When Populists and Democrats fought Republicans in Nebraska in state elections in 1893, both sides tried to seize the statehouse by force, producing the bizarre spectacle of armed militia occupying the chamber while it was still festooned for Christmas.

even stranger for a soldier, he ignored orders. No sooner had the 1864 Democratic Party platform called for an immediate armistice followed by reunification talks than nominee McClellan declared that, on the contrary, the South must seek reunion before the fighting could stop.

Martial law jeopardized civil liberties, and in the depleted Congress the Republicans were able to steamroller through their party platform. Andrew Jackson rolled in his grave as three Banking Acts between 1863 and 1865 ended the era of state banks, and the Legal Tender Act of 1862 added "greenback" dollar bills to America's currency. The tariff was another traditionally partisan issue, but once Southern lawmakers left Washington, Northeastern congressmen raised rates generously for their industrial patrons. By war's end, protective tariffs were twice their 1857 level. For the next fifty years Democrats would attack Republicans over the currency question and the tariff.

Southern Democrats had hoped to share in the speculative possibilities of transcontinental railroad construction and Western settlement. In the South's absence, Republicans chartered the Union Pacific (1862) and Southern Pacific (1864)—despite the name of the latter—to follow a northern route. With their political allies, the two corporations received around 20 million acres of land and $60 million in loans. To accelerate the free-soil settlement, Congress also passed the Homestead Act in 1862 to distribute public land in 160-acre tracts to family farmers. Democrats too had championed westward expansion, but this wartime legislation ultimately produced new Western states that instinctively sided with the Republicans.

The Democrats made gains in the midterm elections of 1862 due to harsh war measures, rampant inflation, and no end to the war itself. Those imprisoned under military law, like Clement Vallandigham of Ohio, seemed always to be Democrats whose crime (to their supporters) was just loudly stating the obvious: The Union could not be forced back together, and the Republicans were passing laws that favored their own. Vallandigham complained in May 1863 that the war was not to save the Union but to free the blacks and enslave the whites. Arrested, court-martialed, and sentenced to imprisonment for the rest of the war, he was instead escorted to Confederate lines on Lincoln's orders.

A lover of the limelight, Vallandigham vainly campaigned for the Ohio governorship from Canada. When he returned to the U.S. in disguise in June 1864, Lincoln shrewdly ignored him. Courting arrest, Vallandigham openly attended the 1864 Democratic National

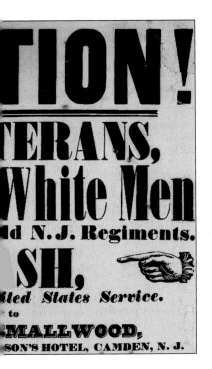

Antiwar Ohio Democrat Clement Vallandigham was put under military arrest in May 1863 and then exiled to the Confederacy. He returned illegally and continued to speak out.

Convention; a foolish move that strengthened Republican claims to be the "National Union" party, with War Democrat Andrew Johnson as Lincoln's running mate. To be fair, Vallandigham was shrewd enough to urge a "New Departure" after the war, but before he could advance that debate within the party, his love of the dramatic proved fatal. As he showed fellow lawyers how a defendant's alleged victim could have accidentally wounded himself, he shot himself through the head. He died on June 17, 1871, the eighth anniversary of his exile.

The Democrats' 1864 defeat was due to timely military victories, and the Confederacy's surrender and Lincoln's murder in 1865 damaged the party's political fortunes even further. Nevertheless, there was a good chance of recovery. Unless steps were taken to prevent it, the return of Southern states to Congress would restore Democratic influence. Ironically, black emancipation, which Democrats had generally deplored, would work to their advantage. The original Constitution had stipulated that House seats would be allocated on the basis of the resident white population plus three-fifths of "all other persons"—in other words, blacks. Once the African American population counted in full, the number of Southern congressmen would rise. At the same time, extending civil and political rights to the freedmen, essential to protect these likely Republican voters from their former slave masters, would involve heated battles in the North as well, where several states blocked black participation. Given the tenor of the times, any backlash could catapult the Democrats back into power.

President Andrew Johnson's rapid readmission plans on the most lenient terms, however, alienated Northern opinion. Georgia's legislature defiantly sent Alexander Stephens, until recently vice president of the Confederacy, to the U.S. Senate. Six of his cabinet colleagues were also sent to Washington, along with four Confederate generals, eight colonels, and innumerable lesser rebels. Simultaneously, Southern state legislatures passed repressive Black Codes to preserve the practical "benefits" of slavery as far as possible. With the South so transparently unrepentant, Northerners in 1866 began to wonder who the victors were.

Reverting to his Democrat roots during the 1866 elections, Johnson attacked the radical Republicans and railed against black citizenship, but succeeded only in alienating moderates. The massacre of African Americans in Memphis and New Orleans in May and July made the moral case for congressional rather than presidential Reconstruction, and Republican election gains gave them enough votes to override any

Black voters kept the Democrats out of power in Southern states until readmission effectively removed voting bans on ex-Confederates, and increased Democratic influence again.

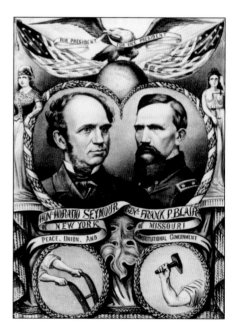

The 1868 Democratic ticket of Seymour and Blair appealed to both farmers and laborers on economic issues, but Republicans whipped up wartime memories in a dirty campaign.

presidential veto or Democratic opposition. In the Fortieth Congress (March 1867–March 1869) the Democrats trailed 8 to 55 in the Senate (Georgia, Mississippi, Texas, and Virginia were still excluded) and by 49 (with independents) to 174 in the House of Representatives.

The fierce struggle to "redeem," as they called it, their states from congressional Reconstruction intensified white loyalty to the Democratic Party in the South, but the party struggled to translate its local support—evident in state election results—into national victories. At the 1868 convention in New York, Southerners foolishly supported the recently impeached and unelectable President Johnson, while Northerners equally unrealistically backed Chief Justice Salmon P. Chase, an eccentric among Democrats because he favored black civil rights. Unable to unite behind anyone after twenty-one ballots, the party drafted New York governor Horatio Seymour. He tried hard to refuse, becoming the first American to receive a major party nomination against his will—small wonder, given the dirty political campaign that followed.

Publicizing the fact that Seymour's father had committed suicide, the Republicans argued that this made the son psychologically unfit for office. They then smeared vice presidential candidate Francis Blair Jr. of Missouri, an outspoken critic of Reconstruction. To counter the Democrats' chant of "Grant the Drunk," a slur the great war hero had stoically endured for many years, Republican newspapers circulated copies of an alleged Blair hotel bill, which listed $10 for board and $65 for whiskey and lemons! Maverick journalist Horace Greeley warned voters: "If you want another civil war, vote the Blair ticket." Even a draining speaking tour by Seymour to show his sobriety, vigor, and good sense could not prevent Grant's 53 percent share of the popular vote, translating into a 214 to 80 electoral college landslide.

During the 1868 campaign, monetary policy and corruption allegations emerged as lasting electoral issues. To the dismay of Eastern financiers, the Democrats had endorsed the so-called Ohio Idea of expanding the money supply by issuing greenbacks to pay off the war debt. This was expected to help farm debt and restrict bond speculation.

When financiers Jay Gould and Jim Fisk tried to corner the gold market in 1869, the currency question merged with a larger issue: Was the American republic becoming corrupt? Neither party was innocent. Southern Democrats charged that the Republican carpetbagger regimes were corrupt, and successive scandals in the second Grant administration deepened factionalism. On the Democratic side, the press pointed to the conduct of William "Boss" Tweed, grand sachem of the Society of

"Carpetbaggers"—Northerners who headed south to seek their fortune during Reconstruction were targets of Southern Democrat resentment, and sometimes violence.

St. Tammany and chairman of New York City's Democratic Party. How could Tweed afford a town house on Fifth Avenue and an estate in Greenwich, *The New York Times*, then a Republican paper, asked, when he only earned $2,500 a year as street commissioner?

Press revelations ultimately suggested that Tweed and his associates had accumulated nearly $200 million in bribes and kickbacks on municipal contracts. The new courthouse had eventually cost $13 million (twice what the U.S. had just paid Russia for Alaska). Its cornerstone, declaimed one critic, "was conceived in sin, and its dome, if ever finished, will be glazed all over with iniquity." Thomas Nast's lethally pointed cartoons worried Tweed far more than any verbose editorial. "My constituents don't know how to read," he complained huffily to one editor, "but they can't help seeing them damned pictures." By 1872 Tweed had been ousted from Tammany and was eventually found guilty on no fewer than 204 counts. He fled to Spain, where a Spanish official recognized him from one of Nast's drawings, and Tweed was returned to New York, where he died in jail in 1878.

Boss Tweed's fall—overseen by future Democratic presidential candidate Samuel Tilden—was not the end of Tammany, of course. By 1870 almost half of New York City's residents were Irish or German immigrants. Maintaining roads, buildings, transportation, and even the semblance of welfare for such a metropolis was a vast and novel task that overwhelmed amateur politics. Only men like Tweed could "fix" it. The Boss provided jobs and helped when a bereaved family wanted to give a loved one a decent funeral. In return, he expected loyalty at election time. Electoral success ensured that legitimate businessmen seeking franchises, permits, and licenses beat a path to Tweed's door, and racketeers gave him a percentage of their earnings to keep the police "sweet." In a society where employers still posted signs saying "Irish Need Not Apply," Tammany Hall maintained its following.

In an attempt to exploit Republican divisions, Democrats endorsed Liberal Republican Horace Greeley for president in 1872. It proved disastrous, but with Boss Tweed's nemesis Samuel Tilden heading the ticket in 1876, there were real hopes that weariness with the Republicans would give the presidency to the Democrats. A firm believer in the gold standard, "Whispering Sammy" Tilden was more corporate lawyer than a spokesman for the common man. He urged civil service reform to end the "spoils system" and tried to exploit revelations of leading Republicans like James Blaine receiving corporate kickbacks.

A wheat bonanza on the Great Plains. Democrats needed to establish themselves in the largely Republican West to address farmers' complaints about railroad rates and trusts.

Samuel Tilden was the unluckiest presidential candidate until Al Gore. He lost the 1876 election after Southern Democrats cut a deal that gave Republican Rutherford Hayes an electoral college majority in return for ending Reconstruction.

Despite concerted Republican attempts to invoke Civil War memories by "waving the bloody shirt," Tilden carried New York, New Jersey, and Connecticut on election day. He won 51 percent of the popular vote, but needed one of three disputed Southern states— Louisiana, South Carolina, or Florida—or even the single disputed elector from Oregon, to push his electoral college total of 184 over the threshold for victory (185). As the 2000 election showed, the Constitution does not specify how to cope with a contested election. If no one wins in the electoral college, then the House votes, and it is the job of the Senate to tabulate the vote. In 1876 gridlock between a Democratic House and a Republican Senate led to the creation of an electoral commission. With ten commissioners from Congress and five from the Supreme Court, the panel was supposed to split seven–seven on party lines with a politically independent justice in the chair. The scheme unraveled when supposed neutral justice David Davis defeated a Republican incumbent senator, thanks to the Democrat vote in the Illinois state legislature. A Republican justice took Davis's place on the commission, and in a series of eight–seven straight party-line votes, awarded Rutherford Hayes victory in the disputed elections, boosting his electoral college total to 185. With the March 4 inauguration date fast approaching, the Democratic House postponed ratification of the result until it had extracted concessions from Hayes. On February 26, 1877, a bargain was struck at the Wormley House hotel in Washington. Republicans promised to withdraw federal troops from Louisiana and South Carolina (signaling the end of Reconstruction) and hinted that there might be federal subsidies for a Southern transcontinental railroad and levies along the flood-prone Mississippi. In return, Democrats dropped their opposition to Hayes's election, and Tilden was abandoned.

Not even selecting a Union Civil War general, Winfield Scott Hancock, could help the Democrats win Northern support in 1880. Even though the Republican candidate, James Garfield, had been implicated in one of the major scandals of the Grant era, Hancock carried only New Jersey among the large, non-Southern electoral college states. The party's dithering on the currency question lost it over 300,000 votes to a third-party candidate in 1880. The Democrats did win in California by endorsing white labor's call for the exclusion of Chinese immigrants. But despite the bands, parades, and posters, the key party plank—that the tariff should be set for revenue purposes rather than as a protectionist measure—was hardly the kind of full-blooded political assault on big business that the enraged strikers of 1877 or angry Western farmers demanded. The latter did manage to force a few state legislatures to pass "Granger laws" to regulate railroad and grain storage rates.

Eventually, however, the Democrats did profit from unflagging Republican corruption. The assassination of President Garfield by a disappointed and deranged office seeker in July 1881 showed how dangerous the spoils system could be, and momentarily chastened, Congress established a Civil Service Commission, although most jobs remained outside its jurisdiction. The mood of repentance passed, and ignoring his public notoriety as a paid agent of the railroads, the Republicans nominated James Blaine in 1884. In contrast, the Democrats chose a clean government candidate, Grover Cleveland. A battling local attorney, he had first attracted attention in 1881 by stamping out graft in Buffalo, New York, and a year later, he continued the fight as governor. Where Blaine was flashy and eloquent, the heavily mustachioed Cleveland was short and stocky with all the earnestness of a minister's son drilled for duty. Like Jimmy Carter after the Watergate scandal, Cleveland seemed the moral man the country needed.

Just before election day, the *Buffalo Evening Telegraph* revealed that the unmarried Cleveland had fathered a child with a rather attractive widow who worked at a local department store. With the election seemingly hinging on the character question, the revelation was dynamite. "Ma, Ma, where's my pa?" waggish Republicans chanted, "Gone to the White House, ha, ha, ha!" Remarkably, Cleveland braved it out, insisting that his party managers tell the truth. He admitted paternity and said that he had provided continuing financial support. Blaine, meanwhile, failed to question his party's description of the Democrats as the party of "rum, Romanism, and rebellion" and by his failure inadvertently rallied the Irish American vote for his opponent. It proved a fatal error, since New York's thirty-six electoral college votes sufficed to carry Cleveland to victory: 219 to 182.

As president, Cleveland belonged to the old Democratic Party. In the Jacksonian tradition, he proved as hostile to special interests as he had been as mayor and governor. He was also committed to Thomas Jefferson's old dictum that the government that governs least governs best, and his philosophy brought cold comfort to those who turned to government for help. He vetoed a bill to aid drought-stricken farmers in 1887 with the words, "Though the people support the government, the government should not support the people." He scrutinized individual

Cartoonists had a field day with "ring" scandals, such as "Whiskey Ring" and "Navy Ring" during the Grant administration. Having failed to capture the White House in the contested election of 1876, Democrats thought they must make a breakthrough in 1880.

Despite having to brave lampoons like this, the unmarried Grover Cleveland was not damaged by revelations that he had fathered a child and went on to victory in the 1884 presidential election.

The skeptical gaze of Mary Lease, the Kansas Populist who rallied farmers in the tumultuous political climate of the 1890s.

veterans' pension claims more assiduously than had any of his Republican predecessors and vetoed a Dependent Pension bill in 1887 that would have extended entitlements. Union veterans were the backbone of the Republican Party in many states, so this was a partisan issue. Partisanship equally meant that as the first Democratic president since 1861, Cleveland was expected not to allow his principles to stand in the way of patronage. Despite doubling the number of protected civil service positions, this did not satisfy the reformers, while it antagonized Democrats hungry for the spoils of victory.

To his credit, Cleveland successfully urged the creation of an Interstate Commerce Commission (ICC) in 1887 to regulate the railroads. But in practice, the courts limited the ICC's authority in ways that threatened corporate interests less severely than had the earlier Granger laws at the state level. Cleveland also attacked the protectionism embedded in the tariff. He proposed eliminating or lowering import duties on over 4,000 items. Such tariff reform might increase access to the U.S. market for British manufacturers, and this possibility paved the way for a highly effective Republican "dirty trick." Under an assumed name, a California Republican wrote to a British diplomat asking his advice on how to vote. In his reply to "Mr. Murchison," published on the eve of the campaign, the minister foolishly hinted that Cleveland would be preferable to the Republican Benjamin Harrison. It was enough to link Cleveland to the British free trade policy and lose him New York. Despite winning the popular vote, Cleveland lost to Harrison in the electoral college: 233 to 168.

With renewed control of both Congress and the White House, Republicans set about rewarding their special interests. Pensions to Union veterans soared, and the McKinley tariff raised rates to an all-time high. At the state level, Republican activists passed temperance laws and required schooling to be in English to the dismay and anger of German immigrants in particular. Unable to ignore public agitation over the plight of debtors and the scope of corporate power, the Fifty-first Congress (1889–91) passed the Sherman Silver Purchase Act and Antitrust Act in 1890. But the resulting mild inflation due to the Sherman Act did little for desperate Southern and Western farmers, and the significance of the antitrust measure was greatly limited by conservative court rulings.

Although the Democrats made gains in the 1890 elections, bolder policies came from a third party—the People's Party, or Populists—with articulate local advocates for farming interests like Kansan Mary Lease.

As farm prices plummeted in the late 1880s, debt repayments and transportation costs ate into the already slender profits of small-scale Western wheat and Southern cotton producers. Farmers felt that while they fed and clothed all other men, they themselves lived on scraps and in rags. So when Populist speakers like Lease in Kansas said the remedy was to "raise less corn and more hell," she found a ready following. Populists proposed an alternate banking system, extending credit on the basis of stored crops, and the public ownership of the railroad and telegraph. To tackle corruption in politics, they urged direct democracy: measures such as popular referenda, the recall of politicians by petition drives, primary elections to select candidates, and the direct election of senators.

The Populist challenge underlined the recurring difficulty of operating the Democratic Party as one party at both a national and a local level. In the Western states, the Populists threatened the Republicans primarily, and this fact prompted fusion with the Democrats in 1892. The Populists traded support for Cleveland as president for support for their local candidates. In the South, the situation was reversed. So-called Bourbon Democrat regimes, rooted in the large plantation districts, faced a Populist challenge of hard-pressed yeoman farmers and sharecroppers. In Georgia, Tom Watson was even bold enough to challenge the color line to induce black Republicans to vote Populist. "You are kept apart," he told black and white farmers, "that you may be separately fleeced of your earnings."

Alarmed, the Bourbon regimes used whatever means necessary to quash the Populist threat. In close contests, the African American vote was crucial and in some cases bought. The tragic aftermath of the Populist defeat was the introduction of various legal restrictions on the right to vote and of racial segregation laws. Aimed at black voters, literacy tests and poll taxes reduced the poor white electorate as well, and when combined with gerrymandering—the artificial rigging of political districts—they allowed a small Black Belt planter class extraordinary influence. To survive politically, even men like Watson became racist demagogues within a faction-ridden Democratic Party.

Returned to the White House in 1892, Cleveland was increasingly unresponsive to the needs of rank-and-file Democrats. His reaction to the deepening depression of 1893 was blindly orthodox, reflecting the gulf that separated the Northeastern party elite from its rural Southern allies. His lack of sympathy for the unemployed and support for employers in the violent industrial disputes at Pullman, Homestead, and

The world's first Ferris wheel at the 1893 Columbian Exposition in Chicago symbolized modernity and a new technology. As the new century approached, the Democrats would find it difficult to capture the progressive new mood—and with it the White House.

Young William Jennings Bryan, a silver-tongued speaker in 1896, was still unable to rally enough Democrat and Populist support to defeat a slick Republican presidential campaign.

Coeur d'Alene stands in contrast to the compassion shown by later Democratic presidents during economic depressions. As gold reserves dwindled, Cleveland called a special session to repeal the Silver Purchase Act. Yet Cleveland's heartlessness was aggravated in appearance by a secret bravery. Concealing the fact that he needed emergency cancer surgery lest it deepen financial panic, the president announced that he was going sailing. With a rubber prosthesis replacing his cancerous upper jaw, Cleveland resumed a full schedule after only five days and cut a deal with the Morgan banking syndicate to boost gold reserves. Ultimately, this proved extremely profitable for J. P. Morgan but left the small farmer and the urban unemployed as desperate as ever. "When Judas betrayed Christ," railed Democratic senator "Pitchfork" Ben Tillman, "his heart was not blacker than this scoundrel, Cleveland."

Simple remedies appeal to desperate people, and in the election of 1896, the elaborate schemes of the Populists were condensed into the basic cry of "free silver." At the Democratic convention, delegates paraded with silver badges and banners and listened spellbound as the thirty-six-year-old Nebraskan William Jennings Bryan urged the party to resist those, like Cleveland, who idolized the gold standard as the anchor of stability. Like a Biblical prophet, Bryan thundered: "You shall not press down upon the brow of labor this crown of thorns, you shall not crucify mankind upon a cross of gold!" The nomination was his, and within days, so too was the Populist nomination, as silverites demanded fusion to defeat the Republican William McKinley. Fusion in the South, fumed Populist vice presidential candidate Tom Watson, cast the Populists in the role of Jonah with the Democrats as the whale.

Free silver, business critic Henry Demarest Lloyd complained, was "the cowbird of the reform movement," laying its eggs in a nest built by others and pushing all the other eggs smashing to the ground. It overshadowed all the other demands of the Populists. Worse still, it did not appeal to the urban worker, who reasonably enough feared that inflating the currency for farmers might simply mean higher prices for him. Sweeping the Northeast and Midwestern states plus California, McKinley secured a two-thirds majority in the electoral college. The last Civil War veteran to stand for president, he was also the first presidential candidate to benefit from modern campaign management. Mark Hanna, observed Teddy Roosevelt, "advertised McKinley as if he were a patent medicine." With Bryan, the Democrats were still relying on that old-time religion, and they would not regain the White House until 1912.

Secession and War

With a distinguished career as a Democratic politician behind him, Jefferson Davis of Mississippi (above) was inaugurated first president of the Confederacy on February 18, 1861. It proved an invidious position for the prickly former senator, who eventually served two years in jail for his part in the rebellion. But in early 1861 prospects were bright. By April 14 South Carolinian batteries had forced the surrender of federal Fort Sumter in Charleston harbor, and the new Confederate flag with just seven stars was raised (right). When Lincoln called upon loyal states for troops, Virginia, Arkansas, Tennessee, and North Carolina added their stars to the Confederacy, greatly increasing its life expectancy. The first Battle of Bull Run in July was viewed as a Southern victory, but it was militarily indecisive and it revealed that ahead lay a war that would break many hearts and homes before it ended.

"Little Napoleon"

The setback at Bull Run prompted Lincoln to promote General George B. McClellan (left, with his commander in chief at Antietam in September 1862) to head the Army of the Potomac. With a flair for parade-ground showmanship and a partisan affiliation to the Democrats, McClellan held himself in high esteem and delighted in his nickname "Little Napoleon." A West Point graduate, he reveled in training and logistics, but seemed always to require more time, more supplies, or more troops before he could advance or pursue the enemy. "If you don't want to use the army," Lincoln wrote him testily, "I should like to borrow it for a while." Given to referring to Lincoln as that "well-meaning baboon," the dismissed McClellan returned to public prominence in 1864 as the "Peace Democrats" presidential candidate with running mate George Pendleton of Ohio. With 45 percent of the popular vote in an election that swung on news of multiple Union victories, McClellan lost to Lincoln and slid into obscurity as a Napoleon who was certainly imperious but not victorious.

Suspected Traitors and Spies

Republicans questioned Democrats' loyalty to the Union and likened them to copperhead snakes that might strike at any time. Mayor Fernando Wood (above) proposed that New York leave the Union in 1861 and operate as a free port. His brother's *New York Daily News* was notoriously critical of the Union side of the conflict and allegedly allowed Southern spies to send coded messages via its personal column. Mayor Wood was also blamed for the violent draft riots that erupted in New York in 1863. Rioters targeted the free black community to ram home their opposition to a war to free the slaves (below right). The famous Confederate spy Belle Boyd (above right) used her legendary charms to further her covert activities—*La Belle Rebelle*, as an admiring French journalist dubbed her. Even when arrested on suspicion of spying, she was able to persuade a Union general to release her.

The President's Assassin

Lincoln's assassin, John Wilkes Booth (above), seemed to confirm Republican fears of Southern and Democratic treachery. He was from a distinguished theatrical family, his brother Edwin being the most famous actor in the country. Knowing her son John's fierce Southern sympathies, Booth's mother made him swear not to join the Confederate army. He kept his word, limiting himself to smuggling supplies out of Washington. In the spring of 1865, however, as the Confederate cause grew desperate, the melodramatic Booth grew desperate and plotted to abduct Lincoln and spirit him away to the Confederate capital of Richmond. The wild scheme failed, the defeated South surrendered, and Booth's fevered mind turned to

murder. Using his familiarity with the venue and his status as a well-known actor, he secured admission to Lincoln's box at Ford's Theatre on April 14, 1865, and shot the president while he was watching a comedy from the comfort of a rocking chair. Booth broke an ankle leaping from the box to the stage but still managed to make his escape. Twelve days later he was tracked to a tobacco barn in Virginia. When he refused to surrender, the barn was set alight and Booth was shot in the neck. He was dragged, mortally wounded, from the barn and died hours later. His final words were: "Tell my mother I did it for my country."

Counting the Dead

Old-fashioned tactics and new
weaponry boosted the fatality rate in
the Civil War, making it the kind of
emotional firestorm that scars an
era. Those who survived Shiloh or
Gettysburg (right) never forgot the
experience, and those who sent
husbands, brothers, or sons, or indeed
all three, remembered forever the men
who did not return. To Peace
Democrats in the North, the price of
enforced union was too high by 1864.
They did not support a war to free
the slaves and instead wanted a
negotiated peace. To Democrats
in the South, the experience of total
war typified by Sherman's 1864
march through Georgia left a legacy
of hatred that would confront
postwar advocates of rapid reunion.
Republicans had become for Southern
whites not just a political party but the
enemy, and for such men, to be a
Democrat was part of honoring one's
fallen comrades. "The past was not
dead," as William Faulkner later
phrased it, "it was not even past."

A Prostrate South

The concluding year of the war, 1865, had been hell for the
South, as Union forces smashed their way through the
Confederacy. The cities of the Old South, such as Charleston,
South Carolina, where the war began (right) and Richmond,
Virginia, the Confederate capital when the war ended
(above), were skirted and pockmarked by ruins. In
Charleston's case, much of the old city had survived, but the
long siege of Richmond left terrible damage. The peace
signed at Appomattox could not instantly clear this rubble.
Reconstruction was therefore a physical as well as a political
process. The occupying Union armies were simultaneously
resented yet needed to create the stability that would allow
repair and recovery. But what most Southerners wanted
in 1865 was a civil society with homes rebuilt, businesses
relaunched, government reconstituted, and hopes renewed.

Life After Slavery

Almost as soon as Union armies advanced into the South, slaves took the advantage to escape their masters. Many worked in Union camps as laborers (left), but their long-term future remained in doubt. The principal skills of such freedmen were agricultural, and to prosper in that work they needed land. Some radical Republicans floated the idea of allocating "forty acres and a mule" to each freed household, the land to be confiscated from Confederates. Democrats and moderates in their own party, however, were united in opposition to such a scheme. The Northern Democrats were equally fearful that unless the freedmen were employed again on Southern plantations, they would migrate to Northern cities and compete for work with white laborers, often immigrant, who were the mainstay of their political support. The black population should remain a primarily Southern, rural workforce in their view, and Reconstruction should ensure continuity rather than change in America's race relations.

The Knives Come Out for Johnson

The need to present his government as one of national unity persuaded Abraham Lincoln to select Tennessee Democrat Andrew Johnson (left) as his running mate in 1864. Less than six months later, Lincoln's murder brought the self-educated and rough-tongued Johnson to the presidency. From a frontier Jacksonian tradition, Johnson's Unionism was fueled by his fury at planter condescension. Initially, his fiery rhetoric of "punishing traitors" made radical Republicans assume that he would depart from Lincoln's plans for rapid reunion. Johnson was equally driven, however, by a racist disdain for African Americans. By December 1865 he had pardoned over 13,000 former Confederates, enabling them to reclaim their lands, and he urged the rapid establishment of new governments. He blocked a civil rights bill and other measures to help and protect the freedmen in 1866, but large congressional majorities overturned his vetoes. By 1867 Johnson's Reconstruction was depicted as a wicked alliance of apelike Irish immigrants, uncontrite Confederate veterans, and greedy New York businessmen, each determined to crush the lives of black Union veterans (above right). To limit Johnson's power as commander in chief, Congress passed the Tenure of Office Act, which Johnson allegedly violated by sacking Edwin Stanton as secretary of war. This triggered the first impeachment of a president in U.S. history (below right), from which Johnson escaped by a one-vote margin. By antagonizing powerful figures and entrenching sectional hatred, however, Johnson prolonged Reconstruction and damaged Democratic prospects.

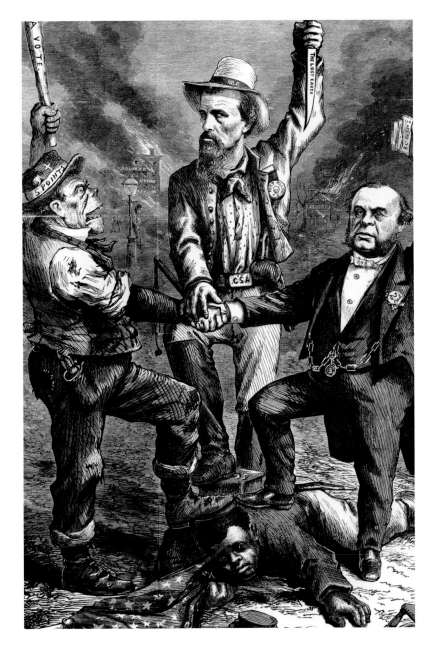

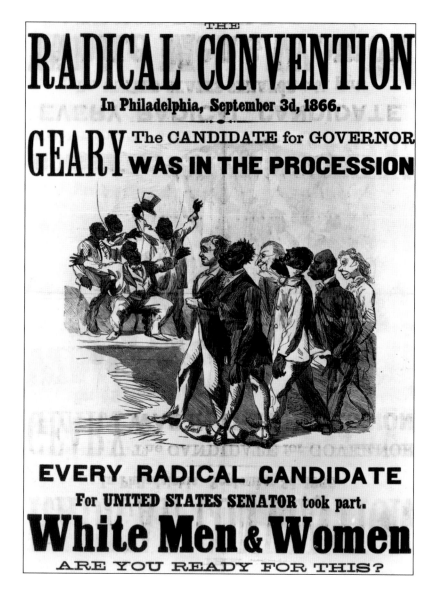

Black Hopes, White Fears

Democratic candidates had used crude racial propaganda before the Civil War, claiming that black Republicans favored racial intermarriage. After emancipation, the same rhetoric was used against radical Republican candidates like John Geary in Pennsylvania (above). The charge that Radical Reconstruction produced inept and corrupt "black rule" in the South was later repeated in history textbooks and not corrected until a "Second Reconstruction" in the 1960s forced a reevaluation of the segregated Southern way of life. Since mainstream white culture denied their dignity and talents, African Americans made a conspicuous attempt to show their respectability in true Victorian style. Fisk University, established after the war, demonstrated African American abilities via the likes of the Jubilee Singers (right), who performed across America and the world, singing not only ornately arranged "slave spirituals" but European parlor songs as well.

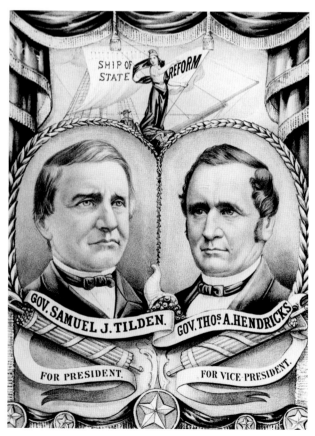

The Scandalous Deeds of Boss Tweed

Through kickbacks and corrupt deals, Tammany boss William M. Tweed (above) controlled postwar New York and enriched himself and his associates. The portly Tweed was a cartoonist's dream, and in the brilliant Thomas Nast, he met his nemesis. Nast pilloried Tweed mercilessly in the course of a lengthy exposé into his crooked deals by *The New York Times* (top left) in 1872. Public opinion turned against Tweed, while at the head of the official investigation into his activities was Governor Samuel Tilden, who gained the Democratic presidential nomination in 1876 (left) largely on the strength of it. The *Times*'s case against Tweed

focused on the cost of the new courthouse (above). The city had spent nearly $13 million—an astronomical sum at the time. It was easy to see why. One carpenter was paid $360,751 for one month's labor in a building with very little woodwork. A furniture supplier received $179,729 for three tables and forty chairs. And most notoriously, a Tammany functionary, Andrew J. Garvey, earned the nickname "the Prince of Plasterers" by securing $133,187 for two days' work. Tweed himself partly owned the Massachusetts quarry that provided the courthouse's marble.

A Democrat in the White House

On March 4, 1885, for the first time since James Buchanan on the same day in 1857, a Democrat was sworn in as president of the United States. Jubilant supporters crowded onto the Capitol steps to see Grover Cleveland make history. He would prove a hardworking and high-principled president, but his orthodox economic beliefs and faith in limited government did not allow him to use his position to consolidate Democratic power. Cleveland would fail to win reelection in 1888, but prove victorious again in 1892, making him the only president to serve two nonconsecutive terms.

Cleveland's Private Side

At first sight Grover Cleveland (opposite) looked like a staid Victorian gentleman with his ample girth and full moustache. But his private life was not uneventful, which was apparent when he confirmed the revelation in 1884 that he had fathered an illegitimate child. Meanwhile, when his law partner Oscar Folsom died suddenly, Cleveland settled his estate and oversaw the education of Folsom's daughter, Frances (above). While she was at college, the rising Democratic politician—twenty-seven years her senior—began wooing Miss Folsom with letters and regular bouquets. Having entrusted social

arrangements during his first year as president to his bookish sister, Rose, Cleveland surprised the press by announcing that he would marry his young bride on June 2, 1886. This first White House wedding caught the public imagination, and the young First Lady was widely admired for her beauty and charm. The couple retired to Princeton, and she was at Cleveland's side when he died in 1908. After a second happy marriage to an archaeology professor at the university, she remained a local celebrity until her death in 1947 at the age of eighty-three.

The Final Land Rush

The settlement of the American West, which was a key factor in destabilizing the two-party system before the Civil War, continued rapidly and dramatically in the postwar decades. Officially, the area of "free" land—the frontier—closed with the census of 1890, and the dramatic rush for claims in the Oklahoma territory in 1893 (right) captured the intensity with which Americans still hungered for their own homestead. Between 1884 and 1896, the number of states in the Union increased from thirty-eight to forty-five, largely because the Republican Party tried to offset the resurgence of Democratic influence in the Senate by admitting Great Plains and Rocky Mountain states, whose assemblies they believed they could control. Ultimately, the race for land in the West affected the race for political power in Washington.

Seeds of Populism

Pioneering on the Nebraskan prairie (above) and sharecropping in the Black Belt of Georgia (right) in the decades after the Civil War was backbreaking and soul-trying. The 1862 Homestead Act allowed any adult citizen to claim 160 acres of public land for the price of a filing fee, provided they improved it and resided there for at least five years. Settler families discovered that surviving on the treeless prairie was a struggle, especially if the railroad owned the best bottomland and drought or pests decimated the crops. First promised and then denied "forty acres and a mule" to establish their own farms, freedmen worked as sharecroppers, sometimes for the same master on the land they had tilled as slaves. In both cases, homesteader and sharecropper needed credit to see them through to harvest in the expectation that their crop would more than cover their debts. By the mid-1880s this was increasingly unlikely as commodity prices spiraled downward. With their profit margin shrinking, farmers grew more suspicious and angry over the charges leveled by merchants and freight companies. In the West they changed a social organization, the Grange, into a political lobby group that pressed for state regulation of rail freight rates. In the South farmers grew so incensed at the cost of credit that they organized a Farmers' Alliance and set up cooperative stores to try to improve their bargaining power. By the early 1890s the alliance had entered politics and was calling for wide-ranging political and economic reform.

Immigrant Labor

After 1880 the regular transatlantic steam ships such as the Red Star Line's SS *Pennland* (left) had their decks crowded with steerage passengers, wrapped in blankets against Atlantic winds because they were too poor to afford cabins. They were part of a new wave of mass immigration, mainly from southern or eastern Europe. Most were young— between fifteen and thirty-nine years of age—and, contrary to this image, male. They came commonly from family-based peasant cultures in which the elderly were honored and unmarried women were chaperoned and protected. The voyage to America was the first sign that such ideals would be tested. Eventual success in America usually involved the reconstitution of this family ideal, hopefully in a more prosperous setting. Economic necessity, however, frequently required the entire family to live and work together in cluttered tenements, like this family of Bohemian cigar-makers in New York City (above). Paid $3.75 for a thousand cigars, they could produce 3,000 a week if they worked from six in the morning till nine at night. Given their willingness to do so, it is not surprising that American cigar-makers campaigned to restrict immigration. Despite such calls, Democrat politicians tended to be more welcoming of new immigrants than their Republican counterparts.

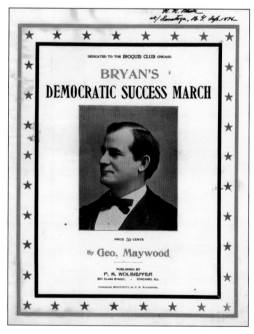

1896: Battle of the Standards

The presidential contest of 1896 was one of the most dramatic in American history. Grover Cleveland, the incumbent Democratic president, had alienated all except a wealthy elite within his own party by his adamant defense of the gold standard and apparent indifference to the plight of the unemployed and dispossessed at a time of severe economic depression. Democrats this time nominated the relatively unknown congressman William Jennings Bryan. The young Nebraskan had electrified the convention with his passionate call for an expansion of the money supply on the basis of the unrestricted or free coinage of silver. This inflationary policy was also demanded by the Populists, who took the unusual step of selecting the Democratic candidate as their own nominee for president. Orthodox economists and Republican supporters of William McKinley, however, saw "free silver" as a prankster's ruse (above) and mocked Democrats for following—perhaps reluctantly—a fool.

Bryan: Modern yet Old-fashioned

Bryan tried to use the latest electioneering techniques: a whistle-stop tour on a campaign train (above) to enable as many voters as possible to listen to his stirring speeches, and a campaign song, the "Democratic Success March" (opposite), to play upon the popular vogue for John Philip Sousa's martial music. The paradox of the 1896 election was that the thirty-six-year-old Bryan ran a more old-fashioned campaign than did his much older opponent, William McKinley, the last elected president to have fought in the Civil War. Bryan was a revivalist with a speaking style that wowed the old rural heartland. With marketing man Mark Hanna at the helm, Republicans ran a disciplined campaign that pulled out their core vote and then told urban workers that a vote for Bryan was a vote for more expensive food. Bryan would lead the Democrats to defeat twice more before they found a genuinely modern, metropolitan candidate.

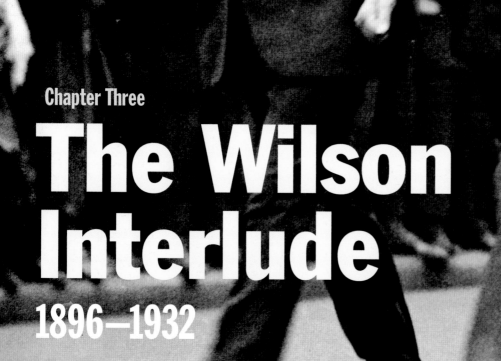

Chapter Three

The Wilson Interlude

1896–1932

The Wilson Interlude
1896–1932

SMARTING FROM THEIR DEFEAT in 1896, Democrats kept faith with the defeated "Boy Preacher," William Jennings Bryan, who, like the Populists, promised to bring government back to the people. Bryan was the party's presidential nominee in 1900 and 1908. But his repeated defeats suggest that the people, then as now, wanted morality sweetened by prosperity. Old issues like the tariff endured into a new century, while new issues such as urban reform also emerged.

Overseas expansion—Hawaii was annexed in 1898—leaped to the top of the political agenda when war erupted with Spain over Cuban independence that same year. Admiral George Dewey soon sent an aging Spanish fleet to the bottom of Manila Bay, and troops landed not only in the Philippines and Cuba, but in Puerto Rico as well. The outright annexation of Cuba was blocked, but the 1898 Treaty of Paris gave America control of the Philippines, Puerto Rico, and Guam. Despite some bipartisan support for Bryan's stance against creating an American empire in the Pacific, the treaty was ratified in 1899, and McKinley won reelection in 1900, with "Rough Rider" Theodore "Teddy" Roosevelt as vice president. Justifying Bryan's fears, U.S. troops faced a Filipino insurrection and remained stationed in Cuba until 1903. When he became president upon McKinley's assassination in 1901, Roosevelt showed himself a dedicated imperialist. He secured the Panama Canal Zone and assumed for the United States international police powers throughout the Western Hemisphere. Despite the patriotic fervor of these years, some Democrats worried that imperialism jeopardized America's traditional neutrality, and others feared a dilution of the white race, whether from the Caribbean or the Orient.

In the buildup to the Spanish-American War, a bitter circulation battle broke out between Joseph Pulitzer's *New York World* and William Randolph Hearst's *New York Journal* with lurid tales of disaster, crime, and scandal. The desired effect was said to be as arresting as "a screaming woman running down the street with her throat cut." Such sensationalism had whipped up American fury over the sinking of the *Maine* in Havana harbor so effectively that it seemed as if the "yellow press" could set national policy. Hoping to benefit from Hearst's

A 1900 lampoon shows William Jennings Bryan blowing up President McKinley's imperialist balloon—a reference to the Democrat's impassioned rhetoric against imperialist adventures.

Previous pages: Flanked by advisers, a flag-bearing Woodrow Wilson marches past cheering New York crowds in 1918. His idealistic foreign policy took America into World War I in 1917, but left a difficult legacy of disillusionment and isolationism for his successors.

HEARST FOR MAYOR

MUNICIPAL LEAGUE NOMINATION
Mark your Ballot in the Circle Under the Scales

Newspaper tycoon and Democratic party backer William Randolph Hearst's political ambitions stretched vainly from becoming mayor of New York to president. Hearst's career inspired the famous film *Citizen Kane*.

Puck

Reform mayor Seth Lowe attempts to train the "Tammany Tiger," but boss Charles F. Murphy stands ready to free Tammany from civil service red tape in this 1903 cartoon.

influence, Democrats elected him party national chairman in 1900, and in 1903 he was elected to the House of Representatives. With newspapers in several major cities, Hearst tried to line up the presidential nomination. But his inadequacies as a congressman and his insensitivity over welfare issues, not to mention his close-set eyes and high-pitched voice, made him an unappealing candidate.

While the media could not go so far as to dictate presidential election results, it displayed a growing ability to champion issues. Mass circulation magazines, like *McClure's*, published muckraking articles on political corruption and corporate wrongdoing. Some scandals related to health and safety at work, providing vehicles for a new generation of liberal Democrats in the industrializing cities. But other favored causes such as temperance and moral reform created problems for a party that traditionally drew a significant part of its support from immigrant neighborhoods where saloons, poverty, and vice were concentrated and to a large extent accepted as a part of life.

The Democratic Party was a curious amalgam of reformers and bosses. Joseph "Holy Joe" Folk, a crusading district attorney in St. Louis, shot to national prominence and became Missouri governor in 1904 thanks to Lincoln Steffens's articles about "the shame" of America's cities. But Missouri was also home to the Pendergast brothers, Jim and Tom, and their classic Kansas City machine. Workers had employment, friendly businessmen got government contracts, and the smooth operation made a profit that filled the Pendergasts' own pockets. Bosses sought a rapport with the voters that sometimes resembled that of modern celebrities and their fans. John Francis "Honey" Fitzgerald used his popularity with Boston's South End voters to reclaim power after a setback at the polls. Defeated by a reform movement in 1907, he campaigned successfully again for mayor in 1910 from a stylish open car at a time when the automobile was still a comparative novelty. "If my car were as big as my heart," he bellowed to wide-eyed urchins, "I'd give you all a ride!" His rousing rallies always ended with a chorus of his signature song, "Sweet Adeline," before Honey Fitz's roadster roared off to another ward.

With a Republican in the White House, the Democrats looked to Congress for leadership. In the House, Missouri congressman James "Champ" Clark was building a reputation as a reformer by challenging Republican abuse of the Speaker's powers. With a Democratic majority in the House after 1910, Clark, now Speaker himself, seemed set to be the party's presidential nominee in 1912. But then at the Baltimore convention, "the Ring-Tailed Roarer," as Clark was nicknamed, could not quite reach the required two-thirds majority. After forty-six ballots the party finally voted for New Jersey governor Woodrow Wilson.

With the Republicans divided between Taft "regulars" and Roosevelt's "Progressives," the Democrats scented victory. In a state whose lenient laws had made it the preferred home for corporate giants like Standard Oil, Wilson had nevertheless managed to push through workmen's compensation laws and public utility regulations. Opposition rarely shook him. "If you want to make enemies," he once remarked, "try to change something." At the core of Wilson's "New Freedom" platform, the antitrust issue enabled Democrats to campaign on the old Jacksonian basis of the People versus the Interests. But Wilson would be a new kind of Democrat, prepared to use the powers of the presidency to establish a more positive role for the federal government. Some later complained that his policy actually was closer to Teddy Roosevelt's "New Nationalism." But, despite lingering suspicions of federal power in the South, the Virginia-born Wilson sensed that laissez faire—leaving everything to an unregulated free market system—was an outmoded conservative position. "A conservative is a man who sits and thinks," he once wrote, "but mainly sits." The time had come for action.

With a landslide electoral college majority of 435–88 over Roosevelt, with just eight votes going to Taft, and also control over both House and Senate, the Democrats took the reins of power in 1912. Through seniority, Southerners dominated congressional committees, and Wilson amplified the region's influence by appointing five Southerners to his ten-man cabinet and retaining Colonel Edward House as his key adviser. A Texan political fixer rather than a real army colonel, House helped Wilson win the nomination. He became Wilson's key foreign policy adviser, first toward Mexico, then toward the European war, and finally during the Versailles peace negotiations.

Shortly after his inauguration in 1913, Wilson summoned Congress into special session to reduce protective tariffs, becoming the first president to address it in person since the second president, John Adams. With a nod toward Bryan, now his secretary of state, he quickly pushed through the Federal Reserve Act to create a more flexible, decentralized monetary system with twelve regional reserve banks, but none of the instability associated with the earlier Populists' schemes. Although Wilson sent the attorney Louis Brandeis, an antitrust campaigner and his political ally, to the Supreme Court, his generally conservative

A symbol of growing Democratic congressional influence, House Speaker Champ Clark lost the party nomination to Woodrow Wilson in 1912, but still helped to pass his reform program.

A powerful speaker, Woodrow Wilson was able to capitalize on his Southern roots and his New Jersey reform record to defeat the divided Republicans in 1912.

appointments to both the Federal Reserve Board and the Interstate Commerce Commission reassured big business. The 1914 Clayton Antitrust Act, another key Wilson reform, gave the semblance of corporate regulation more than the reality. As the 1916 reelection campaign loomed, Wilson shrewdly reassured his reform-minded supporters by securing laws to provide low-interest loans for farmers, to reduce child labor, and to guarantee railroad workers an eight-hour day. On the contentious question of votes for women, the president was no radical, believing that individual states should set franchise requirements. His cabinet colleagues also extended Southern racial segregation to federal agencies to avoid friction between whites and what Wilson unashamedly called "an ignorant and inferior race."

With little or no background in foreign affairs, Wilson nonetheless had very definite opinions, and he insisted that morality rather than expediency guide foreign policy. He apologized to Colombia for Roosevelt's involvement in the Panamanian insurrection in 1903, which was the means by which Roosevelt gained control of the Canal Zone. Foreshadowing his European stance, his schemes to make Mexico "safe for democracy" in the bloody aftermath of its 1910 revolution ultimately led to U.S. military intervention in Vera Cruz in 1914.

When the European war erupted, Wilson judged neutrality to be America's best option. While the economy was booming with war orders from both sides, the war was not popular and neutrality avoided the dangers of conflicting allegiances, particularly among many new Americans. But submarine warfare on the high seas made neutrality hard to sustain. In May 1915 a German torpedo sank the British liner *Lusitania* off the Irish coast with the loss of 1,198 passengers, 128 of them Americans. In the cargo hold there had also been 4.2 million rounds of Remington rifle ammunition, and Secretary of State Bryan suspected the Allies of using civilian passengers as "human shields" for munitions shipments. Bryan resigned when Wilson refused to ban Americans from belligerents' vessels. Demanding an end to the submarine attacks, Wilson nonetheless resisted calls for war with Germany in typically righteous style: "There is such a thing as a man being too proud to fight. There is such a thing as a nation being so right that it does not need to convince others by force that it is right."

In the nation at large Wilson had to face not just the predictable hostility of German and Irish Americans to the British and other Allied powers, but also a growing peace movement that included social

German Kaiser Wilhelm II offers derisory compensation to President Wilson for American lives lost on British ships sunk in the German U-boat campaign.

reformer Jane Addams and suffragette Carrie Chapman Catt. The grief and devastation caused by the male-led war made a very strong case for an equal voice for disenfranchised women as "the guardians of life." Republican strength in the Midwest and Northeast meant that in 1916 Wilson needed to carry several Western states where women could vote. Having sent Colonel House to Europe to try (vainly) to mediate peace, Wilson ran for reelection as the man who "kept us out of war." He won a cliff-hanger—just 1,500 votes in California would have given Republican Charles Evans Hughes victory.

Reinstalled, Wilson urged the warring parties in early 1917 to seek "peace without victory." In a desperate bid to break the stalemate, however, the Germans renewed their submarine campaign to starve Britain into submission, and an intercepted telegram to the German ambassador in Mexico revealed plans for a hostile alliance against America. In response, Wilson addressed a special joint session of the two houses of Congress on April 2, 1917, where he received overwhelming backing for his declaration of war. Wilson insisted that the United States sought no national gains, but the establishment of a more stable international order. His Fourteen Points, which followed in January 1918, included a commitment to open rather than secret diplomacy, to national self-determination, decolonization, disarmament, and most importantly, to a League of Nations to keep the peace.

With the combatants virtually exhausted in Europe, American intervention tipped the balance for the Allies. Particularly in the battles of the Marne and the Meuse-Argonne offensive of 1918, the fresh American troops ensured Germany's defeat. Meanwhile, the Wilson administration pioneered government intervention in economic affairs by taking a strong organizing hand in the home front. The War Industries Board, staffed by corporate executives, proved able to direct many aspects of the economy, but it could not keep the lid on either inflation or labor unrest, and it failed to curb profiteering. By 1920 twenty-three states had active labor parties, and economic migration to major production centers had created racial tensions and housing shortages.

In December 1918 Wilson set sail for Europe to attend the peace conference at Versailles, near Paris. This journey began the tradition that American presidents tour the world to promote their diplomatic goals. The rapturous reception he received in France added to Wilson's already inflated self-importance at a time of deepening political difficulties at home. Despite Wilson's appeal for a large Democratic vote as an

Mexican revolutionary Pancho Villa's raids into New Mexico in 1916 prompted Wilson to send General Pershing into Mexico in pursuit of the "bandits."

Once war was declared in 1917, the Wilson administration used powerful anti-German propaganda to rally Americans.

endorsement of his leadership, Republicans had regained control of both the House and Senate that November. When he decided not to take either Republican senators or senior statesmen like ex-president Taft to the Versailles negotiations, Wilson greatly increased the difficulty of obtaining the two-thirds Senate majority required for the ratification of any treaty. Wilson saw his vision as the framework for peace and he needed the Allies to embrace his plan. But European leaders were skeptical, not least worldly, wily old French premier Georges Clemenceau, who had his own agenda. "God gave us only ten commandments," he remarked drily, "and we broke them. Wilson gives us fourteen points." With a Gallic shrug, he added, "We shall see."

Wilson failed to fulfill the hopes he had raised. The mention of German "war guilt" and the imposition of reparations by the treaty confirmed that this was a peace imposed by victors. Japan secured territory in China, and the principle of self-determination was not applied consistently in Europe, let alone across European colonial empires. For Wilson, concessions were justified to secure the League of Nations. For his critics, however, they simply paved the league's future with potential conflicts that might ultimately demand American lives. To Republicans in the Senate, Wilson had trampled on George Washington's grave and negotiated an "entangling alliance."

In the fall of 1919 Wilson's already fragile health broke during an arduous cross-country tour to whip up popular support for ratification of the League of Nations. Having been rushed back to Washington on October 2, he suffered a stroke that left him paralyzed down his left side. Wilson, with strong backing from his wife Edith, refused to resign. Vice President Thomas Marshall took no action, even though the president was incapacitated and without him the cabinet was not permitted to meet officially. The only business concluded for the next fourteen months was whatever Edith Wilson allowed. She referred to this period as her "stewardship," but critics saw her as a nonelected female president.

In addition to Wilson's illness and Edith Wilson's stewardship, the Democrats faced a nation strained by war. Wheat farmers, for instance, felt that they had lost income due to price controls. Despite these controls, soaring prices had fueled strikes particularly among supporters of the radical Industrial Workers of the World. The "Wobblies," as they were known, joined a long list of groups that government had labeled as dangerously subversive during the war. Congress had passed the Espionage and Sedition Acts in 1918, which gave officials broad authority

Women could vote in several Western states by 1910, a worrying prospect for party bosses back East—and for many other men who feared a reversal of roles.

to crack down on perceived troublemakers. Socialists such as Eugene Debs were imprisoned, and vigilante groups targeted "hyphenated" Americans and radicals. After the Bolshevik Revolution of 1917, a "Red Scare" climaxed in a series of raids authorized by Wilson's attorney general, A. Mitchell Palmer, in early 1920. Wartime propaganda had nurtured prejudice, and in the new decade Democrats found it hard to unite their traditionally immigrant, Northern, urban constituencies with their more commonly native-born, rural Southern Protestant supporters.

The mass migration of African Americans from the cotton fields of the South to the industrial cities of the North met a vicious white backlash. Race riots rocked twenty-six cities in the summer of 1919, notably Chicago and Washington. Amid deepening social divisions, a revived Ku Klux Klan spread from the Deep South to pursue its goal of "native, white Protestant supremacy" against a variety of religious and racial groups, and anyone of whom it disapproved. In the rural Midwest the Klan dispensed vigilante justice against wife beaters, adulterers, and after the passage of Prohibition in 1920, suspected bootleggers. Intolerance was also evident in two immigration restriction laws (1921 and 1924) that limited overall immigration and favored white groups.

The Democratic Party's Northern bastions, like New York City, were founded on immigrant voters, many of them Catholic or Jewish. Having survived the reformers, Tammany Hall was led into the 1920s by the dashing Jimmy Walker. A popular figure in the city with a 1905 hit song and his own record company, Mayor Walker was responsible for establishing the Department of Sanitation, unifying the public hospital system, and pressing ahead with subway construction. Such vital public works had habitually ensured not just the people's well-being but the financial health of the party leadership, and so it proved with Walker. In 1932 he was forced to resign following corruption charges.

The solid South was a Democratic stronghold. By the 1920s political competition there was confined to factions inside the party. Often they reflected a division between candidates sponsored by wealthy economic interests (sometimes called Bourbons) and insurgents (often from former Populist areas) who claimed to speak for the "little man." But single issues, particularly Prohibition, splintered the party. In Texas, Governor James E. Ferguson began a turbulent political career fighting Prohibition at the county level and went on to rally poor white support by calling for rent-control legislation and more spending on rural schools. Ferguson was simultaneously lining his own pockets, however,

Five-time Socialist candidate for president, Eugene Debs was the most famous antiwar dissident to be locked up. Even from prison Debs polled 900,000 votes in the 1920 election.

New York's flamboyant mayor Jimmy Walker gracing the cover of *Time* magazine, January 11, 1926. Walker epitomized the ebullient if morally carefree spirit of the Roaring Twenties.

and was impeached by the Texas Senate in 1917. "Pa" Ferguson, nonetheless, had a devoted following. After unsuccessful bids to return to the governor's mansion or advance to the U.S. Senate, Pa placed his wife's name, Miriam Amanda "Ma" Ferguson on the ballot for governor in 1924. She told Texans that since she would always follow Pa's advice, they should regard this as a chance to have "two governors for the price of one." In November she and newly elected Nellie Ross of Wyoming were sworn in as the first two female governors in American history.

Ferguson-style government did not change, and soon rumors circulated that land and cash had secured prison pardons and highway paving contracts. The Fergusons left the executive mansion in Austin again in 1927, but Ma was elected once more in 1932 and later mustered over 100,000 votes in the 1940 primary election at the age of sixty-five. The Fergusons were just one of many Southern Democratic political dynasties that included the Longs of Louisiana, the Talmadges of Georgia, and the Gores of Tennessee.

After 1910, Northern job prospects and Southern brutality triggered an African American exodus to Harlem, Chicago, and other urban centers.

Local power proved impossible to translate into presidential victories in the 1920s because the great diversity of the party's following afflicted it with a lack of focus—a recurring theme for the Democrats. For a time the party seemed a national joke. Humorist Will Rogers observed, "I am a member of no organized political party. I am a Democrat." The 1924 national convention was deadlocked after 103 ballots, partly due to Klan influence, which blocked the nomination of Governor Alfred E. Smith of New York, a Catholic of Irish stock and an opponent of Prohibition. The exhausted delegates eventually chose a dull congressman, John W. Davis. The huge 1924 defeat left even the normally sunny Franklin Delano Roosevelt pessimistic about prospects for the immediate future. He averred that his party would not recapture the White House "while wages are good and markets are booming."

As the 1928 election approached, the Republicans were confident that they could promise "a chicken in every pot and a car in every garage." They nominated a trained engineer, Herbert Hoover, who may have spoken more often than President Coolidge, the laconic incumbent, but did so in a monotone that could quell the excitement of a lottery winner. Well aware that their own divisions had contributed to the 1924 debacle and free from a diminished Klan influence, the Democrats nominated Al Smith, a gregarious soul who loved campaigning. When a heckler yelled, "Tell them all you know, Al. It won't take long," Smith shot back: "I'll tell them all we both know, it won't take any longer!"

Despite Tammany roots, Smith was a champion of administrative efficiency. As governor he had employed social scientists and women reformers like Frances Perkins to develop social welfare policies in a way that foreshadowed Franklin Roosevelt's brains trust. But this mattered less to rural heartland voters than his Catholicism. As governor he had attended mass daily. And while his support of state divorce legislation may have angered the Catholic Church hierarchy, his opposition to Prohibition alienated Southern doubters. Smith lost by a landslide, with five Southern states voting for Hoover. Smith believed his faith had denied him the presidency. "I guess the time has not yet come when a man can say his [rosary] beads in the White House," he told friends.

Smith's seemingly disastrous defeat, however, actually contained seeds of the coming Democratic majority. He carried the nation's twelve largest cities and attracted many children of the foreign-born, many of whom were casting their votes for the first time. If the Democrats held their urban base and placated the South, they had a formidable coalition, especially if the Republicans were to lose their long association with prosperity. In the summer of 1929 a few shrewd souls, notably the wealthy Democrat Joseph P. Kennedy, liquidated their stock portfolio at the crest of a bull market. Many more did not and watched in horror as Black Thursday (October 24) wiped $9 billion off share values. As the economic crisis deepened, the prospects for the Democrats looked up.

Hoover presided over an increasingly desperate, gloomy, and angry nation. By the time he departed the White House in 1933, one worker in four was unemployed and millions more were on short time and reduced wages. Farmers, whose income had been uncertain even during the booming 1920s, saw commodity prices halve in four years. A million farms were foreclosed. Desperate army veterans marched on Washington in July 1932 to demand early payment of a bonus that had been promised by Congress if they survived until 1945. Camped around the Capitol as the Senate rejected their demands, 2,000 of them—men, women, and children—were driven out by tanks and tear gas on the orders of General Douglas MacArthur. When presidential hopeful Franklin Roosevelt heard of this he told a friend, "This will win us the election."

Near city dumps and along railroad tracks, the dispossessed huddled in makeshift shacks or derelict cars. In reference to the president's apparent indifference, they called their shantytowns "Hoovervilles." The mood of the country was changing, and by 1930 Democrats had won control of the House. With rebel Republicans they could control the Senate. To slow the spiral of bankruptcies and foreclosures, the

Responding to the idea of "two governors for the price of one," Texans elected Ma Ferguson as their first female governor in 1924. They knew her husband, Pa, was still boss.

Immigration restriction laws in 1921 and 1924 reduced the flow of newcomers with quotas that favored northern over southern and eastern Europe, and Europe over the rest of the world.

Democrat-controlled Congress established the Reconstruction Finance Corporation for business loans as well as a discount mortgage scheme for homeowners. As state and local government coffers emptied, Democratic Senator Robert Wagner led the fight to provide direct federal relief for individuals, but Hoover resisted. The federal government should not become directly involved, he insisted. In hard times, self-reliance came first, then private charity, and then, perhaps, local government on a temporary basis. That was, he said, the American way. Nominated for a second term, Hoover entered the 1932 presidential race with an almost palpable weariness and a transparent lack of inspiration.

In 1932 Democratic delegates knew that the man they chose in Chicago was almost certain to be the next president. They selected New York governor Franklin Delano Roosevelt, who had been elected in 1928 at the same time as his predecessor, Al Smith, went down so spectacularly to defeat. FDR's extraordinary ability to convey enthusiasm and hope was captured by his campaign song, "Happy Days Are Here Again," by his pledge of a "new deal for the American people," and also by his exuberant smile and the rakish tilt of his cigarette holder. In the 1920s a self-help guru had preached the doctrine of "mind over matter," and Roosevelt was its embodiment. The polio that paralyzed his lower body in 1921 would have ended the political ambitions of most men. But it seemed to intensify FDR's. With the complicity of the press and even of the public to some extent, he projected an image that denied his disability. Seeing his smiling face, spectators forgot all about the braces that enabled him to stand. One of his Harvard professors remembered him condescendingly as a young man with "a second-class intellect," then adding, "but a first-class temperament." In fact FDR was about to demonstrate one of the most remarkable personas in political history.

With the help of skilled party manager James Farley, he won the nomination, smiling all the while and making few real commitments. He buried Hoover in the November election, and on his coattails the Democrats added control of the Senate to its House majority. The interregnum ensured four long months of deepening destitution and despair. During that time Roosevelt refused to associate himself with any of Hoover's initiatives to cope with the grave economic crisis. By Inauguration Day, Hoover could barely speak for rage, and his scowl played the foil for FDR's dazzling smile. Roosevelt, meanwhile, had pressed his advisers to prepare a veritable bombardment of initiatives ready for launch as soon as he took office.

"Do you inhale?" asks the already notorious chain smoker Franklin D. Roosevelt, in this 1932 cartoon that assumed FDR's leisure-class status made him ill-suited to lead a nation in crisis.

Bryan's Enduring Appeal

The packed 1908 Democratic Convention in Denver, Colorado (above), nominated William Jennings Bryan for the presidency for a third time. He never succeeded, but no failing Democrat has been nominated as often—a reflection of Bryan's enormous personal appeal as well as the party's electoral weakness. Like an evangelist, Bryan (right) captured the hearts of a devoted rural following, but he never appealed as potently to the increasingly crucial urban vote.

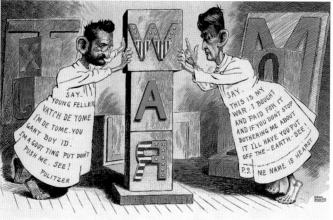

"Remember the *Maine*"

On February 15, 1898, explosions ripped through the American battleship USS *Maine* stationed in Havana harbor (far right). From the crew's (surprisingly) racially integrated baseball team (above right) only J. H. Bloomer (back row, extreme left) survived. The others were listed among the 260 fatalities. President McKinley had ordered the *Maine* to Havana after riots there to protect American interests. William

Randolph Hearst (top left, pictured with son William Jr.), had worsened U.S.–Spanish relations by reporting atrocity stories about how Spain dealt with Cuban rebels. His newspaper rival Joseph Pulitzer had been equally keen to whip up popular outrage. Both yellow press magnates (caricatured far left) pushed for war. They got their wish on April 11, 1898.

"A Splendid Little War"

Compared to Republican enthusiasts like the ambassador to Britain who coined the phrase "a splendid little war" in a letter to his friend Assistant Secretary of the Navy Theodore Roosevelt, many Democrats were uneasy about the war. But the popular mood saw men rush to fight (left) in a war that quickly spread from Cuba to other Spanish possessions including the Philippines. Admiral George Dewey's triumph over the Spanish fleet there gave Americans a hero that they could all share, unlike divisive Civil War figures. A triumphal arch (above) was built in Dewey's honor in New York's Washington Square, and he was briefly touted as a Democratic presidential hopeful.

Shamrock Power

By the early twentieth century, Irish
Americans had proven their gift for politics
in many cities, and the annual St. Patrick's
Day parade (above) was an accepted feature
of the New York calendar. Renowned for his
personal charm, Mayor John Fitzgerald of
Boston, known to all as "Honey Fitz,"
realized that his bond with his constituents
was deepened if he showed that he shared
their passions. When local team the Boston
Braves made it to the World Series in 1914
(right), Honey Fitz (third from the left) seized
the photo opportunity. Wisely, he decided
that a top hat suited him better than an
Indian war bonnet.

1912: Back in Power at Last

Delegates holding tickets (right) for the 1912 Democratic Convention in Baltimore (right) approached the event with renewed hope. The signs for Democrats were encouraging. Recent congressional elections had seen the party's strength grow, and the schism between Republican President Taft and his predecessor Teddy Roosevelt meant that Democratic victory depended on unity. The forty-four ballots suggested that unity would not be easy, but the eventual nominee, Governor Woodrow Wilson of New Jersey, was a political scientist who had written a groundbreaking study of American government. Seated without a hat in a largely straw-hatted gathering (above, just left of center), the bespectacled former professor courted the party's congressmen at his Princeton home in July. The men massed across his lawn would ensure that when he beat the genial Taft (laughing with Wilson on Inauguration Day, far right), he had the votes to pass significant reforms to the tariff, banking, and business regulations.

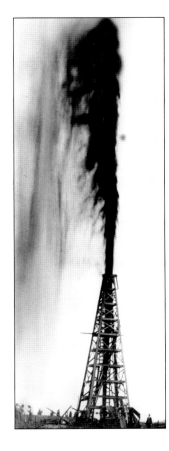

Regulating Big Business

By 1912 the United States had become not just the world's leading industrial nation, but a nation dominated by big business. Large integrated plants like the Homestead steelworks near Pittsburgh (left) dominated entire communities. Tapping natural riches like the Spindletop oil strike in Texas (above left) seemed ultimately to enhance the power of already powerful refiners, the prime example being Standard Oil. As bankers like J. P. Morgan sought security of returns by merging businesses into huge conglomerates, a popular outcry against the power of such trusts prompted attorneys like Democrat Louis Brandeis (above right) to campaign for regulation. During the election of 1912, Wilson championed what he called the "New Freedom." With Brandeis as his mentor, Wilson proposed to regulate business in order to renew competition. Tactics that made it harder for small businesses to compete with corporate giants were outlawed to try to ensure "a fair field and no favors." As a reward for his political support, Wilson nominated Brandeis to the Supreme Court, and he became the first American Jew to hold such a position.

Fighting Child Labor

Cheap labor from the farms of America and immigrants from the Old World spawned a large child labor force in the opening decades of the twentieth century. With nimble fingers to change the spindles and looms in textile mills (top) and bodies well able to scramble through tunnels in the coal pits of Pennsylvania (above), children were prized as laborers. By the time Wilson took office, social reformers were pressing for laws to ban child labor. For the president and fellow Southerners in Congress, there was also the question of how far the government should intervene in what many states jealously guarded as their province. The question was resolved in 1916, when Wilson signed into a law a bill banning the interstate transportation of the products of child labor (right), choking the profit out of child labor without squeezing states' rights too far.

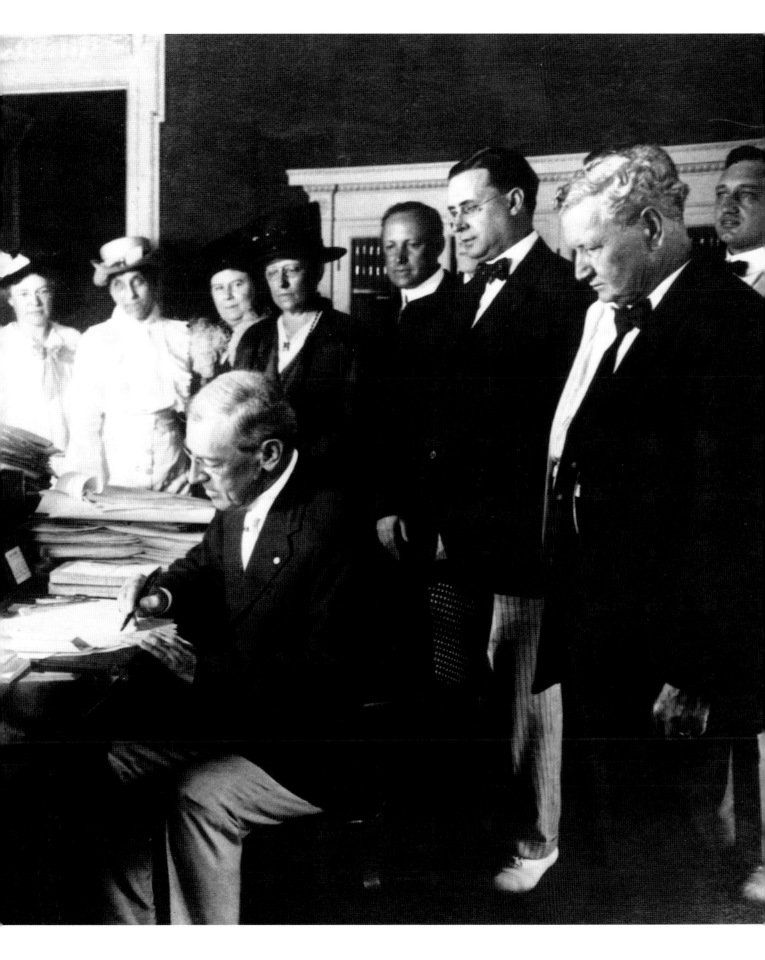

Votes for Women

The demand for women to have the right to vote intensified during the Wilson era. Middle-class, educated women in particular propagandized for the cause (above), sometimes on the basis that they would "purify" politics. But there were always plenty of men who were unsure or opposed (top). The suffrage fight was often linked to other moral reform efforts like Prohibition. This reflected the belief that "Liberty"—as played by socialite Florence F. Noyes in a 1913 suffragette pageant (above right)—was under threat from political corruption. Instead of having to rely on breastplate and helmet, she should be protected by adding pure women to the voting rolls. Like most politicians, Wilson was hesitant to add voters who might go to the polls and vote for his opponent, and it was not until 1920 that women got the vote when the Nineteenth Amendment was adopted.

The Peace Movement

The carnage in Europe strengthened the sentiment for peace. Women were particularly prominent in the peace movement. Well-known figures like pioneer social worker Jane Addams (far right) and suffragette Carrie Chapman Catt (right) founded the Women's Peace Party in 1915.

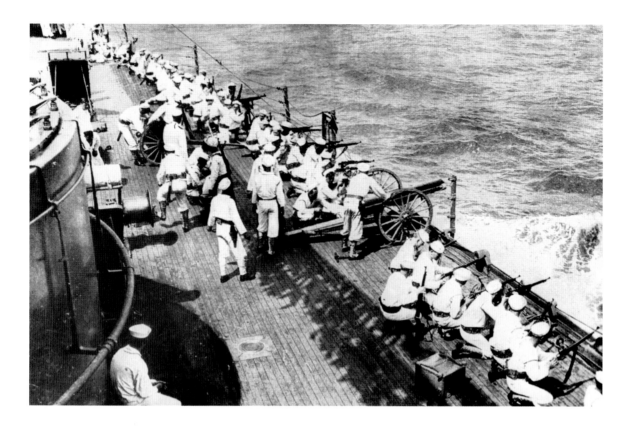

Intervention in Mexico

Determined to "teach the South American republics to elect good men," Wilson ordered the U.S. Navy to bombard and occupy the Mexican port of Vera Cruz in 1914 (above). But "good men" did not include revolutionaries like Emiliano Zapata (left), whose demands for reform in Mexico included land for peasants and caused civil war. Wilson was concerned by the repercussions of the Mexican civil war on U.S. economic interests and the security of the border, and his support for the conservative Carranza faction in Mexico prompted rebel bandit raids into New Mexico, which claimed eighteen American lives in 1916. In retaliation, Wilson ordered General "Black Jack" Pershing (far right) to cross the Rio Grande in pursuit. U.S. troops were successful in capturing some raiders (above right), but Mexican instability continued into the 1920s.

OCEAN TRAVEL.

NOTICE!

TRAVELLERS intending to embark on the Atlantic voyage are reminded that a state of war exists between Germany and her allies and Great Britian and her allies; that the zone of war includes the waters adjacent to the British Isles; that, in accordance with formal notice given by the Imperial German Government, vessels flying the flag of Great Britian, or of any of her allies, are liable to destruction in those waters and that travellers sailing in the war zone on ships of Great Britian or her allies do so at their own risk.

IMPERIAL GERMAN EMBASSY,

WASHINGTON, D. C., APRIL 22, 1915.

OCEAN TRAVEL.

CUNARD

EUROPE VIA LIVERPOOL

LUSITANIA

Fastest and Largest Steamer now in Atlantic Service Sails
SATURDAY, MAY 1, 10 A. M.
Transylvania - Fri., May 7, 5 P.M.
Orduna, - - - Tues., May 18, 10 A.M.
Tuscania, - - - Fri., May 21, 5 P.M.
LUSITANIA, - Sat., May 29, 10 A.M.
Transylvania, - Fri., June 4, 5 P.M.

The Sinking of the *Lusitania*

By 1915 the war in Europe threatened Wilson's stated goal of neutrality. Germany regarded the transatlantic shipping of Britain and her allies as a legitimate target for their submarines, and in the case of the liner *Lusitania* (top left) posted formal notice of this in newspaper advertisements (bottom left). Despite such explicit warnings, 128 Americans died aboard the liner on May 7, 1915, when it was torpedoed and rapidly sank off the coast of Ireland (flag-draped victims, above). Germany insisted that it had obeyed the rules of war, and when Wilson refused Secretary of State William J. Bryan's advice for a ban on Americans traveling on belligerents' vessels, Bryan resigned. Wilson also resisted pressure, however, to go to war. His diplomatic pressure curtailed German submarine warfare—for the time being.

The Campaign Trail

The motorcade had already established
itself as an integral part of the
president's public duties. But the
assassination of President McKinley in
1901, an attempted shooting of Teddy
Roosevelt in 1912, and increasingly
violent labor clashes in Wilson's first
term made the conspicuous bodyguard
an essential presidential motoring
accessory. Wilson always believed that
he could sway minds with his oratory,
and enjoyed the cheers of the crowds.
In 1916 he beat Republican challenger
Charles Evans Hughes by stressing
that he had kept Americans out of
the war. Within months of his
second inauguration, he would
seek a declaration of war against
the Central Powers.

Eat a Peach for Victory

Once war was declared in April 1917, the Wilson government moved quickly to mobilize national resources. By June, over 9.5 million men had rallied to Uncle Sam's call to arms (above) and registered their names. Eventually, 4.8 million saw service of some kind. But war demands also came in unusual forms. The women of Boston (left) pose for a publicity shot to promote the saving of peach pits, a somewhat unexpected component of World War I gas masks.

At the Front

When American forces arrived in Europe, the Allies had a clear and telling advantage. Amid the mud and ruins, simply getting men and supplies where they were needed to be was often a serious problem (above, a typical traffic jam during the Meuse-Argonne offensive in 1918). For the soldiers themselves, the excitement of their initial arrival when they were greeted by cheering British crowds in London (top right) gave way to the horrors of the war itself as they fought their way across No Man's Land (right). About 2 million soldiers served in France as part of the American Expeditionary Force (AEF) under General Pershing. At Chateau-Thierry and Belleau Wood in May 1918, the Americans halted the German advance on Paris. In September of that year 26,000 Americans died in the Battle of the Meuse as the Allies pressed forward. Victory came with the Armistice on November 11, 1918. U.S. war losses had been relatively low compared to the slaughter of European soldiers over a four-year period, but they were enough for America to question whether the peace was worth the cost.

Making the World Safe for Democracy

Wilson's reception as a hero in Europe (above) deepened his conviction that the peace treaty must include a commitment to a new League of Nations to guarantee future international security. In the euphoria of victory on Armistice Day (right, the joyous scene in Philadelphia), hopes were raised that Wilson's idealistic war aims would dictate the peace. But the same crowds that flocked to celebrate peace had just days earlier gone to the polls in midterm elections and dented Wilson's mandate. Voting as much on domestic problems like inflation and industrial unrest, voters returned Republican majorities in both the House and Senate. While Europeans scattered flowers at his feet, Americans were already backing away from the commitments Wilson was agreeing to at Versailles.

Dealing with Dissent

The 1917 Russian Revolution deepened official fears over labor unrest. Boston authorities were so alarmed by the success of the Bolsheviks that they confiscated "subversive literature" (right) in 1919. Across the country, Wilson's hard man, Attorney General A. Mitchell Palmer (opposite) presided over a series of raids that included the arrest and deportation of foreign-born radicals. Wary that antiwar campaigners would exploit tensions within American society, the wartime Wilson administration had already clamped down. Under the Sedition Act, dissidents, especially Socialists, were thrown in jail, and the Red Scare ensured they stayed there, to their families' dismay (above), well into the 1920s.

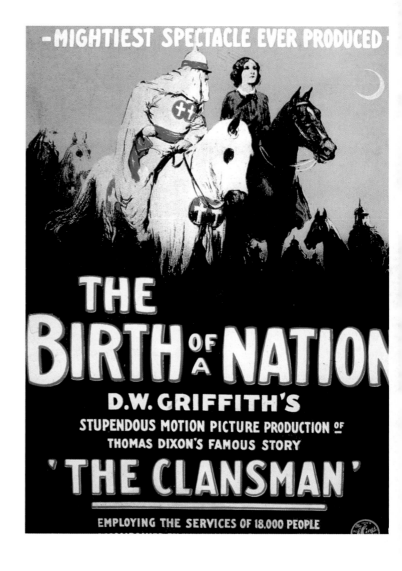

The New Klan

Formed first to defend white supremacy after
the Civil War, the Ku Klux Klan expanded
massively in the First World War era. In 1915
pioneer film director D. W. Griffith celebrated its
first manifestation in his classic silent epic *The
Birth of a Nation* (above right). By the early 1920s
the Klan's trademark burning cross (above) was
ablaze in the Midwest as much as in the Deep
South. The KKK's hate list went beyond African
Americans to include Jews, radical immigrants,
and so-called moral degenerates. At a mass
parade in Washington, D.C., in 1925, men like
Imperial Wizard Hiram Evans could afford to
smile (opposite) as they strutted along posing
as the nation's moral majority.

The "Noble Experiment"

The Eighteenth Amendment, banning the "manufacture, sale, or transportation of intoxicating liquors," became part of the Constitution in 1919. Nationwide Prohibition was put into effect by the Volstead Act a year later. Most states had left the choice to local communities, many of which had already prohibited alcohol for years. Under the Volstead Act, Treasury Department agents had the task of seizing and destroying illegal liquor. In small-town middle America, seizures were small (above), and agents could simply pour the illicit hootch down the drain, but the border traffic in booze offered greater opportunity, as these Brownsville Custom House officials in Texas (right) discovered. Bootleggers ran vast amounts of liquor across the Canadian border, and the traffic made huge profits for legitimate businessmen like Joseph Kennedy as well as outright gangsters like Al Capone. Rural Southern Democrats tended to support Prohibition, whereas Northern urban Democrats felt it should operate on a local option basis.

Al Smith's Defeat

Four-time governor of New York, the brown-derby wearing Alfred E. Smith was a veteran campaigner when he at last got his chance to run for the presidency in 1928. Schooled in Tammany's "get-out-the-vote" tactics, he relished the campaign trail (above, "whistle-stopping" in Chicago). Nonetheless, despite the air of immigrant New York about him, Smith was right at home in the golfing set (right) by 1928, and his final years saw him criticize his Democratic successors. Chief among the latter was Franklin Delano Roosevelt (opposite), whose victory in New York's gubernatorial race in 1928 showed that the 1920 vice presidential candidate was a political force to be reckoned with.

Wall Street Crash

Just months after Herbert Hoover had entered the White House with the promise of further prosperity under the Republicans, the stock market, which had soared to dizzying heights, came down to earth with a bang. On October 24, 1929—"Black Thursday"— panic selling pushed stocks to record lows. After a brief rally, the market tumbled again, and as new record lows succeeded one another, there were lurid reports of overextended brokers who took a final look across Wall Street (left) before ending it all. Companies called in debts, canceled contracts, and laid off workers in droves, which naturally deepened the crisis. Bankruptcies mounted, demand fell, and with limited state relief the jobless had to rely on private charity for food (above, a typical street scene in Los Angeles in 1930). The soup lines of the Great Depression had arrived.

The Bonus March

Congress had promised in 1924 to pay a bonus to surviving World War I veterans in 1945. Desperate veterans caught up in the Great Depression demanded that they get their money now. While the Senate debated their claim in July 1932, veterans from around the country (above, a contingent from St. Louis, Missouri), converged on Washington to protest. After the Senate voted no, over 2,000 remained encamped in tents along the Mall (right). Republican president Herbert Hoover ordered in General Douglas MacArthur, who used tanks and tear gas to drive out the die-hard petitioners. Governor Franklin Roosevelt of New York privately predicted that this brutal action guaranteed a Democrat victory in the November election.

President-elect and Mrs. Roosevelt

An only son with old money, an elegant country estate, and a blue-blood family line sufficiently tangled to allow him to marry his distant cousin, Franklin Delano Roosevelt was not a common man. Educated in establishment citadels—Groton, Harvard, and Columbia Law School—he turned quickly from the bore of law to the buzz of politics. He was a Wilson Democrat and served during World War I as assistant secretary of the navy. At the age of thirty-eight, the handsome, easy-mannered Roosevelt proved sufficiently appealing to the chaotic convention of 1920 to be its vice presidential nominee. When polio struck in 1921, FDR was paralyzed from the waist down and seemingly his public life was over. However, FDR showed unexpected grit, and with leg braces to help him stand and enormous upper body strength, he learned to move again and returned to politics with the same buoyant charm but a new resolve. In 1928, as his predecessor Alfred E. Smith was disappearing under the Hoover landslide, Roosevelt was elected for the first of two terms as governor of New York. As popular discontent with Hoover's inability to cope with the Great Depression grew, the contrast with the confident, bold executive from the Empire State attracted more and more comment. Photographed here in 1929 with wife Eleanor in the gubernatorial mansion at Albany, FDR is characteristically posed to conceal his physical disability. He looks comfortable and confident—the aristocrat who believes he can save a democracy.

Chapter Four

The New Deal

1933–1941

The New Deal
1933–1941

HOOVER'S LAST DAYS AS PRESIDENT saw the banking system near collapse. Good, honest, hardworking Americans had lost everything: savings, homes, and their self-belief, as well as their jobs. Franklin Delano Roosevelt's extraordinary relationship with the American people sprang from his response to this crisis. He reassured them and promised "action, and action now." His optimistic inaugural address bolstered morale, but a more practical and personal appeal to revive trust in the banking system followed a few days later in the first of many radio "fireside chats." After declaring a four-day bank holiday, he told his audience that their money would be safer "in a reopened bank than under the mattress." When the banks reopened, deposits exceeded withdrawals.

In early 1933, before his inauguration, FDR demonstrated his extraordinary resilience. As president-elect he was touring Miami in an open car when a gunman opened fire. The bullets missed Roosevelt but hit Chicago Mayor Anton Cermak, seated beside him. FDR held the stricken Cermak in his arms as the car raced to the hospital and stayed until his party comrade came out of emergency surgery. Understandably shaken by the day's events, Roosevelt's entourage was up all night, restless, and endlessly talking, but not so FDR. He retired at his usual time and slept soundly. Cermak's death a few days later did not dim the new president's unflappable air, suggesting the steel beneath the smile.

Roosevelt's aristocratic good cheer belied an unsurpassed mastery of democratic politics. A distant cousin of Republican president Theodore Roosevelt, FDR had made his way in the rough-and-tumble of New York politics and appreciated the value of party operatives like his New York campaign manager, James Farley. With a phenomenal memory for names and faces, Farley was adept at rallying support and evading criticism. Legend has it that en route to Pittsburgh in 1936, FDR discovered that his speech was supposed to show how he had fulfilled his 1932 election pledges given there, notably to balance the budget and cut the federal government. Having patently done neither, he turned to Farley, asking, "What do I do?" Aware of the public's shallow memory, Farley replied, "Deny you ever said it or that you were ever in Pittsburgh." Appointed postmaster general, Farley freely acknowledged

Radio was a vital new medium for Roosevelt, whose regular fireside chats forged a special bond with the people.

Previous pages: One Big Chief greets another, as campaigner FDR meets Chief Bad Wound at a campaign stop in 1936.

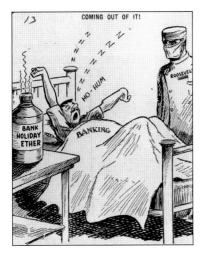

Bank holiday, 1933: FDR's first action on entering office was to close the banks temporarily to stabilize the sickly system. Healthy banks, underwritten by federal deposit insurance, reopened a few days later.

James Farley positioned himself to succeed FDR in 1940 (claiming affinity with an earlier party hero, Andrew Jackson). He felt thwarted when FDR sought and won a third nomination.

that he appointed only loyal Democrats. As such a dedicated party man he believed himself well placed to win the 1940 nomination. To his fury, Roosevelt broke with tradition and sought an unprecedented third term, and the two men barely spoke thereafter.

As president, Roosevelt was more interested in political effect than ideological consistency. Most of all he wanted to maximize support with voters at election time and with Congress in between. With a landslide mandate for action in 1933, he swamped Congress during his fabled first "Hundred Days" with legislative proposals that not only conveyed the impression of activism, but also enabled him to court interest groups and their political representatives. It produced the famous "alphabet soup" of agencies that collectively became the New Deal. The Civilian Conservation Corps (CCC) was one of the first. It provided work for city boys aged seventeen to twenty-four in isolated camps run by the army. While it eased unemployment and crime a little, the CCC was more important as a symbol of FDR's commitment to both work and conservation. Next came the Federal Emergency Relief Administration (FERA), which provided a $500 million boost to state relief funds, although FDR always preferred jobs to handouts. The FERA was quickly followed by the Civil Works Administration (CWA), which in turn became the Public Works Administration (PWA). The last eventually employed more than 3 million people building highways, bridges, public buildings, and parks that served future generations.

One PWA program, the National Youth Administration (NYA), focused especially on youth unemployment and gave one young Texan coordinator, Lyndon Johnson, a lasting taste for government service. Another PWA program provided work for unemployed writers and artists, producing wonderful guidebooks to the individual states and colorful murals in post offices and other public buildings. Still another launched the Federal Theater, which gave a start to such luminaries as Orson Welles. Millions of American families remembered Roosevelt as the president who restored their dignity by giving them work. But the projects—critics charged—made FDR into the king of all bosses and used federal tax dollars to sponsor art that the American public did not want. By FDR's second term, this would produce deepening controversy.

While his true occupation was politician, Roosevelt preferred to call himself a "farmer" and chat amiably about his cotton crop in Georgia. Farmers, the nation's "forgotten men," quickly secured his attention with the 1933 Agricultural Adjustment Act or "Triple A," a comprehensive effort to raise and stabilize farm prices and income by controlling food production. It offered something for everybody involved in the debate over how to maintain farm incomes. Farmers were to be allotted a maximum acreage for each growing season and a subsidy payment to offset any reduction in crop size. With ample scope for local kingpins to allocate acreage in their own favor, the measure was endorsed by powerful Southern and Western congressional figures. Its economic rationale was to boost farmers' spending power and thus demand for industrial products. By stressing the multiplying benefits of using government money to artificially promote economic activity during a depression, it was one of the ways in which the New Deal seemed to follow the new economics of the radically innovative English thinker John Maynard Keynes. It nonetheless created the apparent absurdity of farmers plowing under crops at a time when people were going hungry.

The industrial equivalent of the AAA was the National Recovery Administration (NRA). Cutthroat competition was driving businesses to the wall. The NRA instead tried to set up voluntary cartels to agree on codes of fair competition—for the protection of consumers, competitors, workers, and employers. The NRA was empowered to make voluntary agreements dealing with hours of work, rates of pay, and the fixing of prices. Employers were encouraged to display the NRA's Blue Eagle as proof of patriotism, and with the striking symbol everywhere to be seen in 1933, the NRA made the New Deal look surprisingly like the European fascist regimes, which were similarly keen on suppressing naked competition in favor of imposed agreements. In practice, however, the NRA was too weak to achieve its aims. Employers were too keen to guarantee profits, and few codes were fully implemented. Those that were were often biased. African American leaders complained that blacks lost jobs and bitterly called the NRA "the Negro Removal Act." Like the AAA, the NRA was ruled unconstitutional by the Supreme Court in 1935. Its codes were the equivalent of laws, and Congress, the Court declared, could not give to the executive branch the legislative power that the Constitution assigned exclusively to Congress.

Like much of the New Deal, the NRA was more important for what it symbolized than what it achieved. It was symptomatic of a commitment to wholesale government planning not seen since World War I, and initially it tried similarly to attract business figures into government. When Joseph P. Kennedy was appointed first chairman of the Securities

Displaying the Blue Eagle of the NRA showed that a business was supporting the New Deal scheme to stabilize industrial conditions and prices.

Healthy work on outdoor projects was the hallmark of the Civilian Conservation Corps (CCC), a favorite FDR employment program.

Joseph P. Kennedy, the future president's father, was the first head of the Securities Exchange Commission in 1933.

Exchange Commission (SEC), set up to regulate stock market dealings, many felt it was a classic case of inviting the poacher to become head gamekeeper. Kennedy had amassed a tidy fortune in the bull market of the 1920s, often thanks to insider information. "It's easy to make money in this market," he had famously remarked, "We'd better get in before they pass a law against it." Now that the law was passed, Kennedy quickly reassured his former colleagues that although he knew where the bodies were buried, he would not be "a coroner" dissecting the dead economy. He wanted to restore the confidence of the country in Wall Street and, equally importantly, to restore Wall Street's willingness to invest. Shell-shocked by recent events, a number of major Wall Street banks and innumerable smaller ones were refusing to underwrite new stock issues or loans, no matter how good the collateral or how solid the project. In his brief one-year tenure, Kennedy ended this "strike by capital." It was a typical Roosevelt appointment: It rewarded a key supporter in a way that boosted general confidence, but at the same time denied Kennedy the post of secretary of the treasury that he wanted. Privately, FDR observed tartly that if Kennedy and his fellow financier Bernard Baruch were statesmen, then the definition had changed.

Reporters following Roosevelt's campaign enthusiastically referred to the experts in his entourage as the "Brain Trust." One Trust member was Rexford Tugwell, whom FDR rewarded with a senior post in the Agriculture Department. Tugwell believed that in some communities, the only lasting remedy for social deprivation was the relocation of labor, an idea he pursued via the Resettlement Administration, which tried to establish new communities in which farming and small-scale industry would offer a more secure economic future. This was a radical proposal, which Roosevelt was characteristically prepared to try. If it worked, he would take the credit. If it failed either politically or economically, FDR would have already moved on to other projects.

In many ways, the grandest New Deal project and fullest expression of its commitment to planning was the Tennessee Valley Authority. The TVA encompassed conservation, public utility regulation, regional planning, agricultural development, and the social and economic improvement of the "forgotten Americans." Like so many of Roosevelt's policies, the TVA originated in earlier private proposals, in this case to develop hydroelectric power at the federally owned Muscles Shoals site in Alabama. But the TVA was a far larger project. Its aim was to improve navigability on the Tennessee River, provide for flood control, plan reforestation and the improvement of marginal farm lands, assist in industrial and agricultural development, and aid national defense through the creation of government nitrate and phosphorus manufacturing facilities at Muscle Shoals. Straddling seven disadvantaged states, the TVA held out the promise of a dramatic modernization of the backward South. It also pioneered much-needed rural electrification. Whereas 90 percent of urban Americans had electricity in their homes by the 1930s, only 10 percent of rural families had the same convenience. Thanks to the TVA, countless rural cooperatives, and the competitive response of private utilities, 25 percent of rural homes had electricity by 1939, and the figure climbed rapidly after that. The TVA was soon the largest electricity producer in America, and private utility companies hired corporate lawyer Wendell Willkie to sue it (unsuccessfully) claiming "unfair" competition. Equally unsuccessfully, Willkie would face FDR himself in the 1940 presidential election. Like other New Deal initiatives, rural electrification was an undeniable political asset because it produced tangible benefits for ordinary people, which convinced them that Roosevelt and the Democrats cared for their welfare.

The dams of the TVA were typical of many major New Deal construction projects. Another example was the Boulder Dam on the Colorado River. Roosevelt's dynamic secretary of the interior, Harold Ickes, supervised its completion. His first action was crudely partisan: The giant dam would no longer be named "Hoover" after the recent president, but revert to its original name, "Boulder." More revealing of Ickes's style were his subsequent attempts to boost the construction company's hiring of African Americans. Closer to Eleanor than to Franklin Roosevelt, Ickes was a strong supporter of civil rights and worked closely with Walter White of the National Association for the Advancement of Colored People to establish quotas for African American workers in PWA projects. His efforts met with only limited success. One symbolic blow Ickes struck, however, was in ensuring that Marian Anderson, the wonderful black contralto, could sing before the Lincoln Memorial when the Daughters of the American Revolution refused permission for her concert at Liberty Hall. For this stand and others, Ickes was sometimes called FDR's "liberal lightning rod." His initiatives told FDR how far the public would support liberal measures.

Three out of four African Americans still lived in the South in 1930, where the Depression hit especially hard. But even outside of Dixie, black workers were the last hired and the first fired. Early New Deal

"The Spirit of the New Deal" is the title of this 1933 cartoon by Clifford Berryman, capturing the ideal of the government balancing the interests of employers and employees.

Famed novelist Upton Sinclair mounted an unsuccessful campaign for the governorship of California in 1934. His radical "End Poverty in California" platform called for idle land and factories to be given to the poor.

measures did not help. The AAA's reduction in cotton acreage led to over 200,000 sharecropper evictions, the CCC and much of the TVA were segregated, and the NRA codes incorporated racial discrimination. When the Federal Housing Administration officially classed mixed race or black neighborhoods as "blighted" and strictly limited the number of loans available in such areas, it entrenched ghetto boundaries. Nevertheless, by 1936 FDR had become the most popular president among black Americans since Lincoln and the first Democratic candidate to secure a majority of black votes cast. His relief measures provided a means of survival and a source of hope. His symbolic acts also won approval, notably his willingness to invite black leaders to the White House for consultation. Men such as William Hastie and Robert Weaver were employed as senior figures in Harold Ickes's department, and educator Mary McLeod Bethune served as director of the Negro Affairs division of the National Youth Administration. Collectively, such figures became known as FDR's "black cabinet" or "black brains trust." Anxious not to alienate the powerful white Southern bloc vote, however, the wily Roosevelt rarely publicized these consultations.

Far more than any previous First Lady, Eleanor Roosevelt was a public figure in her own right. Even her plain looks largely worked in her favor. "She ain't stuck up, she ain't dressed up," observed a Maine fisherman approvingly, "and she ain't afraid to talk." An emotional estrangement had followed Eleanor's discovery of FDR's affair with her friend and secretary Lucy Mercer in 1918, but in the struggle to overcome his polio-related disability after 1921, the two forged a formidable political alliance. Eleanor had her own staff, regular press conferences, and access to Democratic party leaders, as well as the president; this enabled her to promote a liberal agenda for both women and minorities. When she asked FDR if he objected to her candidly progressive public remarks on race and women's rights, he said "No," adding with a wry smile, "I can always say, 'Well, that's my wife; I can't do anything about her.' "

Formally, the senior woman in the Roosevelt administration was the secretary of labor, Frances Perkins, America's first woman cabinet officer. Trained as a social worker at Jane Addams's Hull House, Perkins had previously worked on workers' safety issues in New York State and was, Tammany wags claimed, the prime reason why Al Smith had become a social reformer. Brisk and articulate with vivid dark eyes and a broad forehead beneath her favorite tricornered hat, Perkins succeeded in the overwhelmingly male world of politics through dry wit, practical

In fighting the depression, Americans confronted "the moral equivalent of war," claimed FDR, but despite the government's all-out attack, the New Deal found it hard to hit its target.

instincts, and a readiness to beat sense into the heads of men who resisted progress. Despite her best efforts and those of others who shared her commitment, the early New Deal did not ensure lasting, meaningful work for the unemployed or security of conditions and collective bargaining for American workers. Although Democratic majorities in Congress increased after the 1934 elections, it was evident to such social progressives as Perkins and radicals outside the administration that more was needed.

The general economic collapse made Americans more critical of a free market during the 1930s than at any other stage in their history. Thousands joined the Communist Party, which was further strengthened by its public championing of black civil rights. Established politicians such as Governor Floyd Olsen of Minnesota declared themselves socialists and urged the creation of a welfare state. In California Upton Sinclair, a famous socialist writer, won the Democratic gubernatorial nomination in 1934. To fulfill his campaign goal to "end poverty in California," he proposed seizure of the means of production: handing over idle factories and farmland to the unemployed and the poor. While Sinclair went down to defeat, he attracted a substantial 900,000 votes.

Radio priest Father Charles Couglin won support in the mid-1930s by demanding social justice. A fierce anti-Communist, he lost influence by backing fascism and Far Right candidates.

Similarly radical and more seriously threatening to Roosevelt was the flamboyant Louisiana governor Huey P. Long, known affectionately in his home state as "the Kingfisher." Dressed in his trademark white linen suit, orchid shirt, pink tie, straw hat, and two-toned shoes, Long inspired Southern audiences with his oratory. His political machine soon dominated Louisiana. In return for a job with the state, Long expected workers to donate 5 percent of their salary to his campaign coffers and to deliver five loyal voters to the polls. Elected to the U.S. Senate in 1932, Long turned his back on the New Deal two years later in favor of a naive scheme of mass redistribution of wealth. Claiming that as president he could "make every man a king," Long proposed the outright confiscation of fortunes in excess of $5 million and income above $1.8 million per annum. Sharing such wealth around, he claimed, would guarantee every family a house, a car, a radio, and $2,500 a year. For good measure, Long promised qualified students free tuition, the elderly pensions, and war veterans their bonus. Within a year, over 7 million Americans had rallied to Long's banner nationwide.

Long's threat to Roosevelt's position ended suddenly on September 8, 1935, when a relative of a local rival shot Long in the State Capitol Building in Baton Rouge. Unable to wait for a skilled New Orleans

The plan put forward by Dr. Charles Townsend proposed pension payments to the elderly on the condition that they spent their monthly checks in full. He saw this as a way of injecting consumer demand into the economy and jump-starting America's return to prosperity.

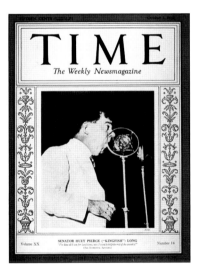

Louisiana senator Huey P. Long broke with the New Deal in 1934 and gathered a huge following for his own radical "wealth-sharing" scheme before being gunned down in 1935.

surgeon, his entourage entrusted the senator's fate to a bungling local surgeon. As he lay dying from internal bleeding, Long's poignant final words were: "God, don't let me die! I have so much to do!"

Other critical voices in 1935 included the "radio priest," Father Charles Coughlin, who resurrected the old panacea of boosting the economy with silver currency, and Dr. Charles Townsend, whose pensions scheme promised simultaneously to cure poverty among the elderly and to boost consumer demand. There were also right-wing critics such as the corporately sponsored Liberty League, which accused the president of promoting "creeping socialism." The emergence of organized labor also played a part in tilting FDR toward the left at this time. The NRA had endorsed collective bargaining, but it had been a generous misrepresentation of Roosevelt's position when John L. Lewis of the United Mine Workers had claimed, "The president wants you to join a union!" Only after workers responded to Lewis's militant appeal and fought violent strikes in Minneapolis, San Francisco, and Detroit did the New Deal truly embrace organized labor. In tandem with New York senator Robert Wagner, FDR pressed for the National Labor Relations Act and had Frances Perkins draft the Social Security Act. He also pressed for a "soak-the-rich" tax bill in 1935 and campaigned in 1936 in the best Democratic tradition as the people's champion.

The result was the most one-sided election since 1820. Only Maine and Vermont rejected Roosevelt, who scooped up over 11 million more votes than Republican rival Alfred Landon. The Democrats also won huge majorities in both the House and Senate. The triumph marked the emergence of the New Deal coalition, combining Northern blacks, organized labor, urban mass constituencies typically of southern and eastern European immigrant stock, and the rural voters of the Solid South. As long as that coalition held, the Democratic Party would dominate and would be most likely to occupy the White House.

The radicalism of the New Deal was always tempered. The Wagner Act of 1935 set up the National Labor Relations Board to curb union militancy rather than fuel it, and the Social Security Act of the same year did not immediately establish a system of state-funded entitlements, but a workers' and employers' savings scheme to pay for future pensions. Social Security also excluded the most needy—farm workers, domestics, and other service sector workers, who tended to be female and black. The measure's immediate effect was to worsen their plight. It took $2 billion worth of spending power out of the economy in 1937. It was the later expansion of Social Security that earned the Democrats a deserved reputation as the party that helps the needy. In a doctrinaire attempt to bring the budget back into balance, FDR unthinkingly worsened the impact of Social Security payroll deductions with tax hikes and spending cuts. The result was a sharp recession in 1937–38, with a 40 percent fall on the stock market and 2 million unemployed.

Men like Henry Ford—who hated FDR—ironically helped him to save his reputation at this point. The refusal of auto and steel executives to accept collective bargaining triggered sit-down strikes in 1937, and their success cemented the Democrats' bond with mass unionism.

Nevertheless, as the midterm congressional elections approached in 1938, FDR seemed to be losing his Midas touch. His proposals to increase the number of U.S. Supreme Court justices and limit their terms in 1937 was seen as a transparent attempt to pack the Court with his own nominees and so end its opposition. It smacked of dictatorship, which was all too visible elsewhere around the world at that time. FDR backed down on his Court-packing plans, and a series of timely retirements allowed him to appoint more sympathetic justices. But he lost further political capital by trying to purge his own party. His relations with the Southern bloc in Congress had soured. They had felt deeply threatened ever since the 1936 convention. Not only had a key guarantee of Southern influence—the requirement that the presidential nominee secure two-thirds of the delegates—been swept away, but black delegates had been seated. After bolting the convention with other Deep South members, Senator Ed Smith of South Carolina declared himself unable to support a party that regarded "the Negro as a political and social equal." They were in no mood to stomach Roosevelt's proposal that as party leader, he should properly manage the 1938 primaries to ensure the selection of liberal candidates committed to the 1936 Democratic platform. They blocked the purge, and FDR's myth of invincibility was damaged. Liberal losses in the November elections weakened his position even further, and former allies like Jim Farley began to maneuver for the succession.

Roosevelt also faced a deteriorating international situation. Ever since the Japanese incursion into China in 1931, it had been clear that without U.S. backing, the League of Nations could not contain aggression. The rise of fascist dictators in Europe—Hitler, Mussolini, and Franco—had confirmed the League's impotence. In the mid-1930s Mussolini invaded the African nation of Ethiopia. Hitler reoccupied the Rhineland, which

Consumer cooperatives were hugely successful in lighting up rural America in the 1930s under the Rural Electrification Administration, but hardly endeared themselves to private utility companies.

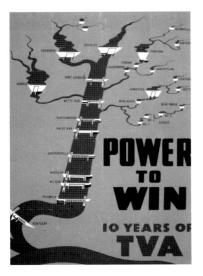

The TVA's success after a decade showed that the federal government could successfully run programs on a huge scale and across state lines.

In the midst of official neutrality, "Lend-Lease" supplied arms to the desperate British in 1940. It kept Britain in the war and ultimately helped bring American public opinion around to the need to face the Axis threat.

had been demilitarized as part of the Treaty of Versailles in 1918. He also gave increasing support to General Franco's forces in the Spanish Civil War. Only a few Americans urged resistance. People still felt hostile to Wilson-style internationalism and preferred isolationism. According to the widely publicized congressional hearings of the Nye Committee, intervention in World War I, however well intentioned, had primarily enriched bankers and munitions makers. The popular sentiment in the mid-1930s was that Uncle Sam should not allow the "merchants of death" to dupe him again. Just as the pragmatic FDR had earlier been prepared to grant diplomatic recognition to the Soviet Union in 1933 in the hope that it would boost trade, he now tried to use the Neutrality Acts to satisfy isolationist opinion, while simultaneously signaling opposition to Japanese and German aggression.

By the late 1930s anti-Communism, which had fed the rise of fascism in Europe, was also reviving in the United States. Influential Catholics in the Democratic Party backed Franco because they feared Communist influence on his Spanish Republican adversaries, which in turn limited Roosevelt's options in this conflict. After his unsuccessful attempts to remove unsympathetic elements from his own party, FDR had to be careful not to provide ammunition for his conservative domestic critics. Congressman Martin Dies of Texas secured establishment of the House Committee on Un-American Activities (HUAC) in 1938 and targeted New Deal agencies, notably the FSA and the Federal Theater, as potential seedbeds for Communist subversion.

With growing opposition to domestic reform and a popular fear that America might be drawn into a fresh European war in 1939, Roosevelt sought an unprecedented third term in 1940. He did his best to respond to the fall of France and the Battle of Britain that summer and traded old destroyers and surplus military equipment for leases on British Atlantic bases ("Lend-Lease"). He hoped to dampen partisan criticism of this move by appointing two prointerventionist Republicans, Henry Stimson and Frank Knox, as secretaries of war and the navy respectively. Despite this maneuver, Republican nominee Wendell Willkie charged that Roosevelt's slanted neutrality toward the beleaguered Allies would mean "more wooden crosses for sons and brothers and sweethearts." Aware of the public fear of war, Roosevelt responded with the promise, "Your boys are not going to be sent into any foreign wars." It was enough for victory, but the margin in the popular vote (27 million to 22 million) was the narrowest since 1916. And, after FDR's unequivocal promise, what would happen if war came?

Rock Bottom

During the winter of 1932–33, while FDR waited to take office, the Great Depression brought millions to the brink of despair. With flat consumer demand, small businesses failed (above) and big businesses laid off workers and cut hours and pay. Deepening farm debt produced an ever-increasing number of evictions with foreclosure sales (right) selling off any remaining items of value. The sheer scale of the crisis was glaring in big cities like New York (opposite). The experience of joining the line for the charity soup kitchens scarred people's pride. Their confidence was gone.

LINE FOR
1¢ RESTAURANT
20 MEALS FOR $1
DONATIONS INVITED
HELP FEED THE HUNGRY
1¢ WILL FEED 20
1¢ RESTAURANT
107 W 43rd ST.

Nothing to Fear

Chief Justice Charles Evans Hughes administers the oath of office to FDR (right) on March 4, 1933, launching the longest presidential tenure in U.S. history (1933–45). To the right of the podium, ready to assist his paraplegic father in the tricky task of walking from the stage, stands James Roosevelt, and on the extreme right, an understandably, but perhaps typically, glum-faced Herbert Hoover. FDR's confident inaugural address broadcast to an expectant nation (above) made his infectious optimism patriotic. America, he declared, had "nothing to fear but fear itself."

Brain Trust

As governor of New York, Roosevelt faced the challenges of the Great Depression by calling on the best expertise he could find. As president he was equally confident that his Brain Trust would provide him with innovative ideas for the "bold experimentation" the grave situation required. He appointed the nation's first female cabinet member, Secretary of Labor Frances Perkins (left), to make use of her welfare expertise to help the jobless. He gave the liberal Harold Ickes, poised (below) to clear a new housing site with dynamite, charge of the many projects of the huge Interior Department.

The Farmer: the "Forgotten Man"

Agriculture had not really shared in the 1920s boom. When the Depression hit, farm debt was already critical, and the angry farmers felt the nation did not appreciate their toil (right). Many of the poorest Americans worked the land for low incomes, like these seasonally employed Connecticut tobacco harvesters (below). The Agricultural Adjustment Act of 1933 tried to tackle farm poverty primarily by limiting production to boost prices, combined with subsidies. Roosevelt believed that a stable rural economy was vital for overall recovery.

Working for Conservation

The Civilian Conservation Corps (CCC) was one of several early New Deal programs influenced by the experience of World War I, and it offered a clear model for concerted state action. Young urban unemployed men in the CCC looked and were treated like army recruits (left), as they carried their kit bags to work camps that were in fact run by U.S. Army officers. As in the wartime army, the CCC typically took recruits (above) away from home (in this case from Idaho to Tennessee). Regardless of their work experience, they were put to work planting trees or clearing land. By merging their varied backgrounds, the process sought to forge a common corps spirit. In later years, many CCC veterans had fond memories of the experience.

FDR and the "Strenuous Life"

Like Teddy Roosevelt, his Republican namesake and distant relative, FDR advocated conservation and believed that the discipline of physical outdoor work was character building (right). The CCC was a Roosevelt favorite, and other cabinet colleagues shared his enthusiasm. Among those enjoying an alfresco meal with FDR at a camp in Virginia's Shenandoah Valley (above) are Harold Ickes, seated second to the left of the president, and to the right, Agriculture Secretary Henry Wallace and planning enthusiast Rexford Tugwell.

The Repeal of Prohibition

As proof of how the Depression transformed
American politics, Prohibition—which had been
one of the reasons why Americans rejected
"wet" Democrat Al Smith in 1928—was repealed
with little controversy on December 5, 1933.
The patrons of Sloppy Joe's Bar in Chicago
(right) predictably celebrated with drinks on the
house. Other Chicagoans, such as notorious
gangster Al Capone (above), were unlikely to be
smiling since repeal dropped the bottom clean
out of the lucrative bootlegging trade.

"Old Iron Pants" and the NRA

Cutthroat competition worsened the impact of the Depression and prompted the New Deal to launch a huge voluntary scheme, the NRA. Under the leadership of "Old Iron Pants," General Hugh Johnson (left), large and small businesses were asked to agree on codes of practice in their sector, which would fix prices and working conditions. The NRA supported labor union membership and banned child labor. The public was asked to patronize only businesses that displayed the Blue Eagle (above). Because it was a voluntary scheme, the NRA relied on Johnson's forceful personality to persuade businesses to sign up and also on a barrage of publicity that included this picture of the NRA triplets: Margaret, Ann, and Eileen (opposite).

Building a New America

Many of the New Deal schemes to provide employment came under
supervision of the Public Works Administration. From the Bonneville Dam
in Oregon (above, under construction in 1936) and the Lincoln Tunnel
connecting Manhattan and New Jersey (bottom right, just after it opened in
1937) to the Triborough Bridge in New York City (top right), the PWA left
monuments to civil engineering that are still in use today. By controlling
floodwaters, generating electricity, and spanning straits and sounds, the PWA
embodied a technological confidence that renewed America's faith in progress.

TVA: Taming Nature

The Tennessee Valley Authority epitomized the New Deal belief that science and technology could master nature, limit her destructiveness, and harness her power to improve people's lives. The farmers of the Mississippi Valley had endured not just droughts that left them destitute (right), but floods that washed away their homes (above). The TVA would regulate the watershed across seven states with dams like Fort Loudon (top).

The Dust Bowl

"Dry farming" the Great Plains had so
loosened the soil that by the 1930s, the
region was vulnerable to devastating dust
storms like the one enveloping a crossroads
town in Baca County, Colorado, on Easter
Sunday 1935 (right). The Dust Bowl and the
westward migration of farmers ruined by
it provided the theme for the novel *The
Grapes of Wrath* (1939) by John Steinbeck
(above). With eerie aptness, as congressional
hearings on soil conservation began, a
monster cloud dumped tons of western
dust on Washington itself, making the
case for conservation more effectively
than any politician could.

"Okies" and Other Migrants

The farm crisis forced farm families off the land. The most famous migrants were the Okies, so-called because they originated from Oklahoma, although in fact they came from many Western and Southern states. The Depression extended the scale and scope of a migration that had been a feature of American agriculture for decades. Seasonal farm labor had long been used on the Texas cotton frontier (opposite), and tenant farmers across the South (bottom left) had often felt obliged to move on. In the Depression decade, however, the scale of the problem escalated so rapidly that the federal government felt forced to respond by setting up camps for migrant workers (center left), while at the same time many migrants gave up looking for land to rent or steady work across the South. They pinned their hopes on the California dream and headed west in old cars with whatever possessions they had (top left).

The First Lady

Before Eleanor Roosevelt arrived on the scene, the First Lady's public duties were largely ceremonial. Here she is fulfilling such a role during the visit of the British monarchs in August 1939 (above). Eleanor played the part well, even if she was a little upstaged by George VI's glamorous wife, Queen Elizabeth (mother of Queen Elizabeth II). Legend has it that FDR entranced the shy young king, keeping him up drinking and talking late into the night before leaning across, giving him a fatherly pat on the knee, and saying, "Now young man, time for you to go to bed."

Eleanor's Wider Role

With her own staff and regular press conferences, Eleanor Roosevelt was a public figure in her own right in a way no previous First Lady had ever been. She could still perform routine ceremonial tasks such as christening the new ship *America* (above), but she seemed more in her element demonstrating her social concerns, for instance by serving soup in a soup kitchen (right) or, more controversially, by championing equal government aid for African Americans (top right).

The 1936 Landslide

The Philadelphia national convention (an entrance ticket, center right) selected FDR as party nominee without hesitation in 1936, and the president crisscrossed the country, defending his record in Western states like Colorado (top right) that had not favored the Democrats since Bryan's day and urging ethnic voters to back the party for other offices by voting a straight ticket (left). In November, it was not just New Yorkers (bottom right), but the electors in every state bar Maine and Vermont, who pulled the Democratic lever to back the New Deal coalition.

Packing the Court

Most of the nine U.S. Supreme Court justices in 1937 (above) were Republican appointees. Opposed to a liberal construction of the Constitution, they had struck down such key New Deal measures as the AAA (top left) and NRA. Emboldened by his recent election victory, FDR proposed Supreme Court expansion (bottom left), adding justices and forcing retirements ostensibly to enable the Court to handle more business, but clearly to pack it in his favor. Uncharacteristically, the president badly misread the public mood and there was a backlash against his proposals. But the Court ceased overturning key measures, and in the next four years, retirements allowed FDR to appoint seven new justices and make the Court his own.

African Americans and the New Deal

In 1936 FDR became the first Democratic president to receive a majority of black votes. This was largely due to his relief measures, but also to his willingness to include men like William Hastie (top left) in his administration and consult with race leaders such as Walter White of the National Association for the Advancement of Colored People (center left) and educator Mary McLeod Bethune (bottom left). Eleanor Roosevelt and New Deal officials like Harold Ickes were far more committed fighters for racial equality than FDR, who was inclined to placate the white South. When the Daughters of the American Revolution refused to allow the black contralto Marian Anderson to sing at Liberty Hall in Philadelphia, Mrs. Roosevelt resigned in protest from the organization. With the assistance of Harold Ickes, whose Interior Department had responsibility for national monuments, she arranged for Anderson to give an Easter concert from the steps of the Lincoln Memorial (right), a move that ironically strengthened the flow of black loyalty away from the party of Lincoln.

The Rise in Union Militancy

A new industrial unionism movement arose in the 1930s (above), particularly in the auto, mining, rubber, and steel industries. It was different from the old unionism of the American Federation of Labor (AFL) because it organized all workers, not just the skilled. It wanted an end to the open shop (left), which employers had used to keep individual workers in a weak bargaining position. In 1937 the autoworkers union (UAW) took on General Motors. Workers occupied the key body-making plant (above left) in a sit-down strike to demand a closed shop with no nonunion "stool pigeons." After a long struggle, GM conceded.

Battle of the River Rouge

Old-style bosses like Henry Ford were determined to have no unions in their factories. Paternalistic when times were good, Ford had adopted strong-arm tactics to quell labor unrest in the Depression years. When a UAW delegation led by Walter Reuther (above, hand on hip) tried to enter the massive River Rouge complex in 1937, company security barred their way. Before the union representatives had a chance to leave, Ford's thugs beat them up (left). It was not until 1941 that Ford joined GM and Chrysler in recognizing the UAW as the collective bargaining agent for all autoworkers under the terms of the 1935 Wagner Act. By that stage the UAW was a key part of the Congress of Industrial Organizations (CIO), whose political action committee was a vital part of the New Deal coalition.

Social Security

The human costs of the Great Depression had underlined the need for some kind of safety net to help ordinary people in hard times. The dramatic loss of savings spurred the case for a national pension scheme that resulted in the 1935 Social Security Act. Beginning in 1937, workers and employers would pay Social Security contributions that would guarantee workers a monthly check for the rest of their lives from the age of 65 (above right). Social Security's chief architect, Frances Perkins, had earlier fought for workmen's compensation laws and she now ensured that widows and dependent children would receive benefits if the family breadwinner died (above).

FDR's Pragmatism

When Roosevelt signed the Social Security bill on August 15, 1935, with Senator Robert Wagner looking on over one shoulder and Labor Secretary Frances Perkins looking over the other (left), he knew that the measure was imperfect. It was a regressive tax: The more you earned, the less proportionately you paid. It excluded many low-income groups like agricultural workers and domestics, who desperately needed a secure pension and insurance scheme of some kind. The workers who signed up (below left) would receive no immediate benefit and actually have less money to spend. But this was all Congress was prepared to pass, and FDR was more interested in action than perfection. Once they had passed this bill, he told associates, and acknowledged that the government should care for the elderly, widows, children, the disabled, and the temporarily unemployed, they would find it hard politically to go back. In time, meager benefits would grow into significant entitlements, an electric rail that cautious politicians would not dare touch.

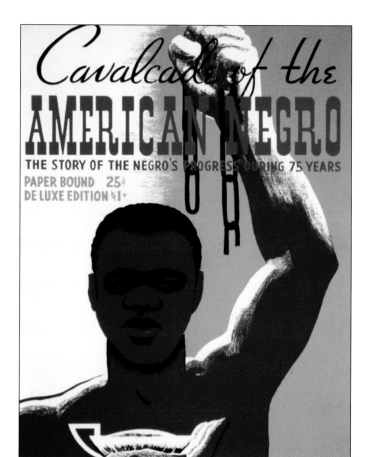

Art and the New Deal

The New Deal's Public Works Administration (PWA) sponsored the arts at a time when the Depression restricted private patronage. Artists such as realist painter Thomas Hart Benton (*Time* cover) and his protégé the then unknown Jackson Pollock (above left, sitting on Benton's front porch) benefited under the scheme. So too did actor-director Orson Welles (above, talking to colleague Agnes Moorehead). Under the PWA umbrella, the Works Progress Administration (WPA) sponsored Federal Art Project exhibitions (opposite, top left). Public buildings such as post offices and schools were decorated with murals that often featured historic figures. In Roosevelt Public School in Roosevelt, New Jersey (opposite, bottom right), artist Ben Shahn puts German-born physicist Albert Einstein in a crowd of immigrants to show the value of transplanted Americans. The project sometimes addressed controversial topics such as African American achievement (opposite, top right) or employed radicals like then-Communist Richard Wright (left). This emboldened conservative congressmen to target the PWA as their influence grew after 1938.

The American Way

Critics such as the business-sponsored Liberty League accused Roosevelt of destroying the "American way." Herbert Hoover claimed the New Deal had weakened American individualism and bred dependency. This jeopardized, he claimed, the free enterprise system that had given Americans the world's highest standard of living. Others saw the New Deal as a savior of capitalism. As other nations embraced fascist dictatorship or Communist totalitarianism, the New Deal provided a potent, liberal alternative. The New Deal tackled problems too big for individuals, but left ample room for individualism. When Soviet leaders showed the movie *The Grapes of Wrath* (1940) to demonstrate capitalism's failure, they were dismayed to find the audience was more impressed that the American poor had cars. The best propaganda against Communism, FDR once remarked, was a Sears Roebuck mail-order catalog. This photograph by the celebrated photojournalist Margaret Bourke-White makes the powerful point that life is not all joy in America, with black flood victims in Louisville, Kentucky, lining up in 1937 to get food and clothing from a Red Cross relief station in front of a famous billboard.

Under Attack from the Left

The Great Depression should, in theory, have been the moment of which Communists dreamed, the time when capitalism failed. Although the vast majority of Americans shied away from the Reds, Marxist ideas did secure an important foothold among intellectuals in the 1930s. The Communist Party adopted a more American vocabulary, speaking of "the people" rather than "the proletariat" and trying to rebut the old charge of being un-American (opposite). The reaction to the Left, however, was at least as important as the Left itself. By the late 1930s liberal groups were accused of being front organizations for Communists (above), and Texas congressman Martin Dies (above left) had secured the establishment of the House Un-American Activities Committee (HUAC) in 1938 to investigate subversion.

Under Attack from the Right

Hitler and FDR came to power at almost the same moment, and by FDR's second term the threat of Nazism was becoming impossible to ignore. Although World War I had seen the repression of German immigrant culture, ethnic Germans remained a large and potentially cohesive group, as the marching men of the German-American Bund (right) demonstrate during an outing from the notorious Camp Siegfried in Yaphank, New York, in 1937. There were many such marches and meetings to protest FDR's attempted boycott of Nazi Germany. While few in number, American Nazis (above, at a rally in 1935) did their best to emulate the puffed up style of their hero Adolf Hitler.

The Pursuit of Neutrality—Up to a Point

As the willingness of both fascist regimes in Europe and the militarist imperial government of Japan to use armed force against their neighbors became undeniable in the late 1930s, FDR wrestled with the twin dilemmas of neutrality and preparedness. Initially he backed neutrality, since it bought time to improve U.S. military defenses. By September 1939, however, he had concluded that the Nazi assault on democratic regimes in Europe posed such a grave threat that he addressed Congress requesting that the Neutrality Act be repealed (above). Public opinion, as demonstrated by the Senate mail room (left), however, was divided, with probably a slight majority hoping that America could somehow remain isolated from the European war.

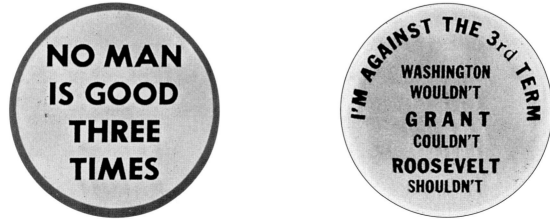

Winning a Third Term

The Constitution in 1940 contained no term limits for the presidency, but the established pattern was retirement after two terms. Doubts about the legitimacy of FDR's third term bid are neatly captured in these campaign buttons (below left), but equally evident is Roosevelt's relish for the campaign as he throws out the first ball of the 1940 baseball season (left). The Washington Senators were taking on the Boston Red Sox, and while the president looks his usual confident self, on this occasion the confidence was misplaced—the ball struck a *Washington Post* camera! He was also keen to establish liberal leadership of the Democratic Party, and gambled that his established appeal with voters would allow him to dispense with the traditional Southern running mate normally expected of Northern Democratic candidates. He chose his liberal secretary of agriculture, Henry Wallace of Iowa (above left), to replace John Nance Garner of Texas. Aware of the strength of isolationist opinion inside his own party, the Republican Wendell Willkie (campaigning above) was also mindful that the deteriorating international situation made that position increasingly untenable. He was outmaneuvered when FDR promised not to send Americans to fight in European wars and was able to make play of his own great experience of the highest office.

The Roosevelt Magic

Franklin Roosevelt was arguably the best-known president in American history, in the sense that people felt they really knew him, what he was like, what made him tick. This was partly a consequence of his boundless enthusiasm for meeting members of the public and charming them as only he could do. FDR also realized how a selective release of "candid" photographs could cement his image: in Indian headdress on home ground in Dutchess County, New York (left); munching a hot dog with the premier of New Brunswick on a beach at Campobello Island, his beloved Canadian retreat (above); and sailing off that tranquil haven (right).

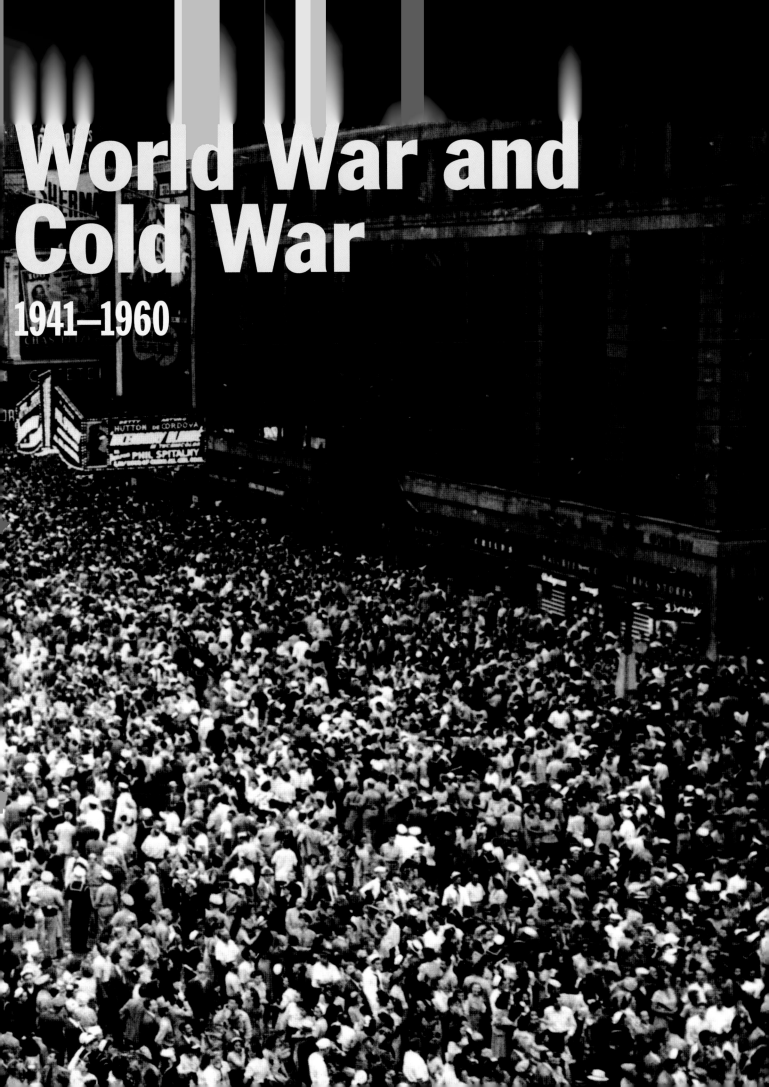

World War and Cold War

1941–1960

World War and Cold War
1941–1960

FRANKLIN ROOSEVELT'S UNPARALLELED twelve years in power and his leadership in both war and economic crisis place him among the greatest of all American presidents. He was certainly a master politician. Aware of the presidential nomination hopes of his ambassador to Great Britain, Joseph Kennedy, Roosevelt profited from a series of damaging leaks regarding Kennedy's "defeatist" attitude to Germany in the summer of 1940. By the time the ambassador returned home in November, he was no longer a political threat. With a popular pledge to keep Americans out of European wars, Roosevelt defeated Wendell Willkie in 1940. Knowing FDR's ultimate belief in the inevitability of intervention, Willkie snapped that he was a "hypocritical son of a bitch!" By the time FDR sought election for a fourth time in 1944, Americans were fighting in both European and Pacific theaters. The possibility of complaint about FDR's broken promise, however, had been sunk by the Japanese attack on Pearl Harbor on December 7, 1941.

The Japanese intention was clear. In a bold attempt to wipe out the Pacific Fleet, in two hours their planes sank nineteen ships, destroyed 150 planes, killed over 2,400 Americans, and put an end to isolationism. The next day, with only Representative Jeanette Rankin dissenting, Congress approved Roosevelt's declaration of war. Bound by treaty to Japan, Germany and Italy declared war on the U.S. a few days later. The American people found themselves again involved in a world war.

Faced with a neutralist Congress, FDR previously had been more combative toward Japan than Germany. Even the increasing persecution of the Jews by the Nazis had not swayed congressional isolationists. When 900 Jewish refugees tried to disembark in Florida in June 1939, they were fatefully turned away. It took the Nazi-Soviet Pact in August and the German invasion of Poland in September 1939 to persuade conservative Southern Democrats to back arming the Allies so that they could fight as America's surrogates. Even after the fall of France and the Battle of Britain in 1940, isolationist opinion tied FDR's hands significantly. Safely reelected, he told America that she must become "the great arsenal of democracy" and asked Congress to approve Lend-Lease arms sales to beleaguered Britain. Over bitter opposition, the scheme

The Day of Infamy: Daybreak on December 7, 1941, as a Japanese aircraft carrier crew cheer and wave their caps at the planes taking off to bomb the U.S. Pacific Fleet at Pearl Harbor.

Previous pages: Crowds fill New York's Times Square to read news of the Japanese surrender on V-J Day, August 14, 1945.

passed in March 1941, escorted convoys left port, and naval clashes in the Atlantic ensued, but did not escalate to war. Only Pearl Harbor—"a day which will live in infamy"—could unite America for war.

Like Pearl Harbor, Hitler's attack on the Soviet Union in June 1941 changed the war's complexion. With his senior advisers Cordell Hull and Henry Stimson, FDR shared British prime minister Winston Churchill's view that the Soviet Union could exhaust the Third Reich in a land war of attrition, in much the same way "Mother Russia" and "General Winter" had drained the armies of Napoleon. Having agreed idealistic war aims of collective security, economic cooperation, national self-determination, and freedom of the seas in their 1940 Atlantic Charter, the Anglo-American leaders met again in early 1943. In Stalin's absence, they endorsed three military initiatives: to end the submarine threat to Atlantic convoys, to "island hop" against the Japanese in the Pacific, and to attack "the soft underbelly of the Axis," as Churchill called it, which meant invading Italy from North Africa. Stalin's demand for a "second front" in Western Europe to reduce the military pressure on Russia was ignored. FDR's sop to "Uncle Joe" was a commitment to "unconditional surrender," which precluded separate negotiations with the enemy. By the summer of 1943 Allied successes encouraged Churchill and FDR to promise a second front to Stalin at their first joint meeting in Tehran. The Soviet Union would enter the war against Japan once Germany surrendered. Winning the war was paramount, but each strategic decision had ramifications. When peace came, ethnic Americans deplored the Soviet domination of their Eastern European homelands, an outcome that eroded their support for the New Deal coalition.

Roosevelt told his advisers candidly in 1942 that "Dr. Win the War" had replaced "Dr. New Deal." Labor shortages—not unemployment—were now the big problem, as defense contracts rapidly expanded production. Millions, recently destitute, now enjoyed a better life. They left isolated rural areas and flocked to industrial centers, but despite the party's proven urban appeal, full employment did not guarantee Democratic success. Thousands of Southerners, black and white, settled in New York, California, Illinois, Michigan, and Pennsylvania, the states that had become the key presidential election battlegrounds. Clashes at military bases and riots in Detroit, Harlem, and Los Angeles highlighted the racial tensions that segregation, overcrowding, and competition over jobs and housing generated. The race question further aggravated the Democratic Party's long-standing sectional divisions.

The sneak attack succeeded in crippling the Pacific Fleet, but it was equally successful in mobilizing the American people behind the war effort.

Unlike Eleanor Roosevelt, FDR had never championed liberalism on racial matters. He had, admittedly, issued an executive order requiring nondiscrimination from defense contractors in 1941, but only after black labor leader A. Philip Randolph had threatened a mass march on Washington. Bowing to popular panic, Roosevelt interned more than 110,000 Japanese Americans in 1942 in one of the gravest infringements of civil liberties in American history. Able to "afford" the progressive Henry Wallace as his running mate in 1940, he dumped him four years later, selecting instead Harry Truman of Missouri—someone whom the discontented Southern bloc could mistake for one of their own.

Roosevelt tried the remedies of increased government expenditure and expanded state economic planning more extensively during the war than he ever had during the New Deal. From mid-1940 to September 1944, $175 billion worth of government contracts were awarded, mostly to the top 100 corporations. At the same time, attempting to guarantee uninterrupted production, the government backed collective bargaining in return for no strike pledges. Organized labor's 8.5 million members supported FDR in 1940. With nearly 15 million members in 1945, they were an increasingly important constituency and expected Democratic leaders to reverse antiunion legislation passed after the 1943 strikes.

FDR funded the war partly through taxes, but the national debt still rocketed. Centralized powers to distribute resources and check prices, however, prevented this deficit from driving unsustainable inflation, and this gave credibility to the idea that the government could manage the economy. By 1945 liberal Democrats conceived of the economy as an uneasy alliance between Big Government, Big Business, and Big Labor, while many Southern Democrats favored a smaller federal government, small businesses, and no closed shops. On race, party unity was fragile.

During the war, more women took paid work outside the home. Challenging gender stereotypes, they became welders, crane operators, toolmakers, shell loaders, cowgirls, police officers—all symbolized by "Rosie the Riveter." Of the new women workers, 75 percent were married and most were over thirty-five, a reversal of the prewar pattern. Just as G.I.s returned home with a wider experience of the world and ambitions that they hoped the government would help them to fulfill, so the daughters of Rosie the Riveter developed career goals that ultimately forced the Democratic Party to tackle the issue of sexual discrimination.

Roosevelt was less strong politically in 1944 than he had been at the war's outbreak. Southern Democrats and Republicans had forged a formidable alliance. They opposed FDR's "Economic Bill of Rights,"

Price controls were more effective in World War II than in World War I and strengthened the idea that government could effectively control the economy.

"Win the War" became FDR's priority in 1942, and his cabinet colleagues are here warned to leave New Deal goals behind.

guaranteeing every American a decent job to provide adequate food, shelter, clothing, and financial security in illness, old age, or temporary unemployment. The successful D-Day landings in Normandy in June 1944 and the liberation of the Philippines nearer election day both signaled imminent victory. With a moderate Republican, Thomas Dewey, challenging a visibly aging FDR, Democrats faced a close contest. But fearful that hard times might return with the Republicans once war contracts were terminated, the voters chose Roosevelt again.

Churchill, Stalin, and FDR met one last time at the Black Sea resort of Yalta in early February 1945. The Soviets' final offensive against Germany had begun, and renewed American advances along the Rhine were imminent. In frail health and determined to ensure that the Soviet Union joined the war against Japan and committed itself to a United Nations security organization, FDR made concessions that reflected the leverage that Stalin had, thanks to his troops' established position in Poland and eastern Germany. Roosevelt's sudden death on April 12, 1945, was part of the difficult legacy thrust upon Vice President Harry Truman. "I don't know whether you fellows ever had a load of hay or a bull fall on you," the new president told reporters the next day, "but last night the moon, the stars, and all the planets fell on me."

Truman had not been part of FDR's inner circle and he had neither his own faction within the Democratic Party nor an established national profile. Party bosses had approved his selection in 1944 largely as a spoiling tactic. Years later, a reporter recalled the contrast between the patrician Roosevelt, who "looked imperial," and Truman, who "looked, acted, and talked—well, like a failed haberdasher," which is precisely what he had been before entering politics in 1922. But the combative Truman would not be a mere caretaker seeing out the fallen hero's term. He replaced much of FDR's cabinet and, barely two weeks into the job, threatened to end U.S. aid to the Soviets unless they allowed free Polish elections. The Red Army's capture of Berlin on May 2 and the formal German surrender on May 7, 1945, strengthened Stalin's position further, but it also reinforced Truman's suspicions. By the time he joined Churchill and Stalin at the Potsdam Conference in the summer of 1945, Truman had been briefed about the successful test-firing of a terrible new weapon: the atomic bomb. If this could accelerate victory, save American lives, and limit Soviet ambitions, Truman was prepared to use it. On July 26 the Allied leaders demanded the Japanese surrender or face "prompt and utter destruction." When no surrender came, the first

Atlantic Charter: Meeting on the British battleship *Prince of Wales* in August 1941, FDR and Prime Minister Churchill watched an aerial display before signing an agreement to jointly defend essential freedoms.

atomic bomb was dropped on Hiroshima on August 6; three days later a second obliterated Nagasaki. The Japanese accepted American peace terms on August 14, but the Soviets remained uncowed by the awesome new weapon as the chill in relations with the Western Allies deepened. So even as peace was celebrated, there were grave concerns for the future.

Early in 1946 Stalin warned fellow Communists that there could be no lasting peace with capitalism, and George F. Kennan, a senior U.S. diplomat in Moscow, wrote his "Long Telegram" outlining the need for an ongoing policy of vigorous containment, given the USSR's inherently "expansionist tendencies." With Truman beside him, Winston Churchill told a Missouri audience that an "iron curtain" now divided Europe, and with Republican support, Truman rapidly persuaded Congress to fund the Marshall Plan to aid devastated Europe and fight Communism. Inside the Democratic Party, former vice president Henry Wallace opposed Truman's "get tough" stance. By mid-1947 Wallace's Progressive Citizens of America was formed, and when he barnstormed the country, 200,000 people turned out to hear him call for cooperation with the Soviet Union. Other liberals in the party, including Eleanor Roosevelt, saw Truman as an unworthy successor to FDR and formed Americans for Democratic Action. Unlike Wallace's Progressives, the ADA accepted the "containment doctrine," and came to represent cold war liberalism. Through figures such as Minneapolis Mayor Hubert Humphrey, the ADA also fought for black civil rights, a stance that sharpened the mistrust evident among white Southern Democrats as the 1948 convention loomed. Truman had already alienated this important wing of the party by demanding the elimination of segregation from American life and issuing executive orders in 1948 against racial discrimination in federal hiring and segregation of the armed forces.

The Republican-controlled Congress had blocked Truman's Fair Deal proposals for a minimum wage and federal aid for education and housing, and had overridden his veto of the Taft-Hartley Act, which barred the closed shop and limited strike action. They attacked Truman's failure to tackle shortages, inflation, and industrial unrest. "Got enough meat?" went a Republican gibe, "Got enough houses? Got enough inflation? Got enough debt? Got enough strikes?" Party activists feared that only drafting war hero Dwight Eisenhower would keep them from losing the White House. With Wallace running as a third-party candidate and Southerners bolting the convention in outrage at Humphrey's successful fight for a liberal civil rights plank, Truman seemed doomed in 1948.

The Manhattan Project drew the best scientists and engineers from all over America to create the atomic bomb that destroyed Hiroshima (above) and Nagasaki. This was to be a forerunner of much government-funded weapons research.

George Kennan: His "Long Telegram" from the Moscow embassy in 1946 outlined a policy for containing Soviet expansion that became central to Truman's foreign policy.

A surprise victory was conjured from Truman's own shrewdness and some Republican complacency. He cultivated the farm lobby and organized labor and played his Democratic rivals off against each other. The Dixiecrat revolt and Truman's fighting speech in Harlem secured significant black support in key electoral college states, and recognition of the new state of Israel won Jewish votes. A tough stance against the Soviet blockade of Berlin, Red Scare tactics against Wallace's Progressives, and a willingness to probe for Communists in government mitigated the "soft on Communism" charge. Republican Thomas Dewey stayed at home trying to offend no one, while plainspoken Harry campaigned nationwide against the "no-good, do-nothing" Republican Congress, emerging as the battling little guy rather than the smug incumbent. The popular vote was close, but victories in key states gave Truman 303 electoral college votes to Dewey's 189.

The Red Scare tactics that Truman partly initiated came back to haunt his second term. In 1948 the House Un-American Activities Committee was already investigating one of FDR's aides at Yalta, Alger Hiss—a spy, according to former Communist Whittaker Chambers. The investigation's driving force was a young California congressman, Richard Nixon. The sensational case climaxed after the election, when Chambers not only produced State Department documents allegedly supplied by Hiss, but also took investigators to a Maryland pumpkin patch. There, from the carcass of a hollowed-out pumpkin, he produced four rolls of microfilm containing secret State Department documents that he said Hiss had smuggled to him in the 1930s. Too much time had elapsed to allow an espionage trial over these 1930s allegations, so Hiss was charged with perjury. The support Hiss, a Harvard man, received at his highly publicized trial from eminent associates like Secretary of State Dean Acheson and Supreme Court justices Felix Frankfurter and Stanley Reed, deepened the suspicion that ordinary Americans in the heartland were at risk of betrayal by effete East Coast intellectuals.

Communist successes fed this fear. In 1949 Mao's Red Army triumphed in China, and with some help from their spy network, the Soviets successfully exploded an atomic bomb. Prominent left-wing figures like African Americans Paul Robeson and W. E. B. Du Bois had their passports revoked, and HUAC grabbed headlines investigating Hollywood. Wisconsin Republican senator Joseph McCarthy claimed in early 1950 to have evidence that Communists had infiltrated the State Department. Simultaneously, Communist North Korea's invasion of South Korea suggested to the credulous that a devious scheme for

Dapper Dean Acheson, Truman's secretary of state, helped to form NATO, but was smeared after supporting Alger Hiss in Hiss's 1948 perjury trial.

Communist domination was unfolding. In the guise of a United Nations "police action," Truman sent U.S. forces to fight in Korea under General Douglas MacArthur. MacArthur drove the Communists back and advanced to the Chinese border before Chinese reinforcements sent his UN forces reeling. By January 1951 both sides were dug in around the original truce line, and Truman offered to negotiate. When MacArthur tried to foment a full-scale war with China, Truman recalled him. The unrepentant general came home to a hero's welcome, and the chances of a Democratic victory in 1952 diminished further. The dismissal of nearly 250 IRS men for corruption that year and General Eisenhower's embrace of Republicanism killed off any lingering doubts.

The Democratic contender in 1952 and 1956 was Adlai E. Stevenson. Erudite and witty, Stevenson looked and sometimes spoke like a college professor. Targeting McCarthy and Nixon, he bravely promised to "talk sense" and "tell the truth to the American people." It was not a standard the Republican camp shared. The GOP's vice presidential candidate, Richard Nixon, asked voters whether they could trust "Adlai the Appeaser," an egghead who had earned "a Ph.D. from the Dean Acheson College of Cowardly Communist Containment?" Stevenson responded, "If the Republicans will stop telling lies about us, we will stop telling the truth about them." But neither Adlai's wit nor the self-deprecation evident in the remark, "In America, anybody can be president. That's one of the risks you take," could overcome the powerful attraction of Eisenhower's combination of geniality and experience. By carrying five Southern states, Ike also suggested that at last two-party competition in presidential races had returned to Dixie. More generally, Democratic successes in state and congressional races revealed a trend for voters to vote a split ticket. From 1954 onward, Eisenhower faced a Democratic Congress.

The old methods of party management were fraying as American life changed dramatically during the 1950s. Pent-up demand for housing produced a suburban boom that eroded the political sociology that had long underpinned Democratic abilities to get out the vote in densely populated ethnic urban wards. Once campaigns had hinged on the efforts of local party captains like Frank Sinatra's mother in Hoboken, New Jersey. By the late 1950s televised campaigns wooed voters with photogenic candidates endorsed by stars like Frank himself. Continuing migration boosted the significance of California and two other Sunbelt states, Texas and Florida, as electoral swing states. As yet another New

As a Progressive candidate in 1948, the former vice president Henry A. Wallace urged détente and civil rights, but he was hurt by Communist Party support.

After speaking out against Truman's foreign policy, the great singer Paul Robeson, who made no secret of his Communist sympathies, was blacklisted.

A battered party but an unscathed candidate. After the divided 1948 convention, scandals, and the Red Scare, in 1952 weary Democrats drafted witty governor Adlai Stevenson of Illinois as their nominee.

With a smile for everyone, the young vice presidential hopeful John F. Kennedy put down a political marker at the 1956 convention—to be picked up four years down the line.

South emerged, Southern New Dealers like Senate Majority Leader Lyndon Johnson of Texas and Senator Estes Kefauver of Tennessee shed the strong sectional image espoused in the Deep South. The reaction of Deep South senators like James Eastland and Richard Russell to the Supreme Court's controversial school desegregation rulings in 1954–55 underlined the differences. Johnson, Kefauver (Stevenson's 1956 running mate), and Kefauver's fellow Tennessee senator, Al Gore Sr., refused to sign the segregationist Southern Manifesto.

With Democratic support, Eisenhower continued a foreign policy of containment. Having kept his promise to end the Korean conflict, Ike orchestrated Senate action against the demagogic Joseph McCarthy, whose own appeal plummeted once audiences saw him on televised hearings in 1954. The mood was one of consensus, with Democratic support on foreign affairs being matched by Eisenhower's reluctance to scrap New Deal programs. In 1956 Ike's health was in doubt after a heart attack, and the Democrats aimed their fire chiefly at Nixon. Partisan exchanges sharpened, however, during Ike's second term. The Soviet launch of the satellite *Sputnik* in 1957, combined with a sharp recession and corruption scandals, created the impression of an elderly president and jaded administration running out of steam. The Democrats held the House 282 to 154 and the Senate 64 to 34 after the 1958 elections. Nevertheless, it would not be easy to prevent Ike's enduring popularity from helping Nixon succeed him as president.

The loquacious Senator Hubert Humphrey was one Democratic hopeful for 1960. Lyndon Johnson, famed for his legislative adeptness, and defense expert Stuart Symington were also contenders. But all three were destined to lag behind the charismatic millionaire senator from Massachusetts, John F. Kennedy. By beating Humphrey in the West Virginia primary, Joe Kennedy's son calmed doubters who feared that, like Al Smith in the 1920s, the Catholic Kennedy would alienate Protestant rural voters. Carrying the convention easily, Kennedy made Johnson his running mate to limit any Southern defections. Tanned, healthy, and confident beside the wan, pained, anxious, and sweaty Nixon in the first-ever televised debate, Kennedy secured a marginal advantage. By engineering the release of civil rights leader Martin Luther King Jr. from a Georgia jail, he maximized his black vote in key states. When Richard Daley's Chicago machine delivered Illinois for the man columnist Joe Alsop described as "Stevenson with balls," Kennedy had scraped into the Oval Office in the closest election since 1888.

Attack on Pearl Harbor

Japanese warplanes left the USS *West Virginia*, the USS *Tennessee,* and many other vessels ablaze early on the morning of December 7, 1941. Despite the devastation, the vital U.S. aircraft carriers happened to be safely out to sea, and by failing to destroy oil tanks and other shore installations, the Japanese ensured that the base could be restored to full operations again in short order. Meanwhile, the sneak attack outraged as it horrified Americans, and President Roosevelt gave full voice to his and the nation's fury at the Japanese malice.

JAPAN'S AGGRESSOR: ADMIRAL YAMAMOTO

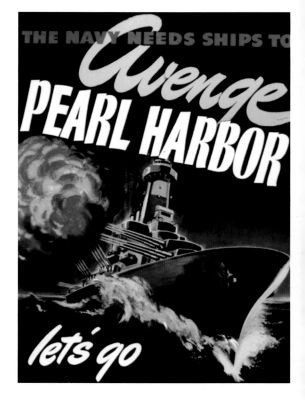

A Resolute Response to "the Day of Infamy"

Wearing a black armband to mourn the Pearl Harbor dead and with colleagues noting the exact time at which the declaration took effect, President Roosevelt signs the declaration of war against Japan on December 8, 1941 (right). Fulfilling treaty obligations, Japan's Axis partners, Germany and Italy, declared war on the United States, obliging FDR to sign a second declaration against them three days later. Amplified by public fury over the surprise attack on Pearl Harbor, the fight against the Japanese was always likely to be shaped by racist antagonism toward the Japanese, as illustrated by *Time*'s cover portrait of Admiral Yamamoto, who planned the attack (above). Popular hostility was still seen as a potent incentive on the home front (above right) even when the war was well advanced.

A Shameful Episode

Revulsion at Pearl Harbor fueled suspicion of Asian Americans, particularly in California, where the bulk of Japanese Americans lived. Their protestations of loyalty (center right) were not believed. Demands for their forcible removal were widespread and quickly heeded (top right). Small businesses like this dime store (bottom right) had to be sold. In February 1942 the federal government ordered all Japanese Americans to assemble for relocation to one of ten internment camps (left). The camps resembled prisons with cramped quarters and poor food. The U.S. Supreme Court upheld Roosevelt's order in two cases challenging the internment. The president did not rescind the order until late 1944, and the camps were not closed until the end of 1945. Compensation, first in 1968 for the loss of property and then finally in 1988 for infringement of civil rights, was eventually granted to the victims.

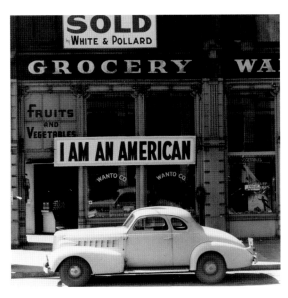

A Busy Time on the Home Front

The Roosevelt administration oversaw the transformation of American industry into "the arsenal of democracy." Workers were urged to work overtime to hit high production quotas to support American fighters at the front (above left). Women workers were encouraged to emulate Rosie the Riveter (above), and consumers were induced to recycle aluminum products to limit domestic demand for a key war material (left). Giant new industrial plants such as the Douglas Aircraft plant at Long Beach, California (right, where the factory workers are singing the "Star-Spangled Banner"), employed thousands to produce planes for the war effort.

The War in Europe

The November 1943 Tehran Conference (above) was the first summit attended by Soviet leader Joseph Stalin. The failure to authorize a second front in Europe to ease German pressure against the Soviet Union had fostered Stalin's mistrust. To mollify him, FDR accepted Soviet demands for at least a temporary partition of Germany after the war and punitive reparations. The Allied invasion of Normandy—better known as the D-Day landings—in June 1944 launched the final phase of the war in Europe (left). By that stage the Red Army was already advancing into eastern Europe, establishing an occupation there that would distress Americans of eastern European origin for decades after the war.

The Pacific War

The war against Japan began to turn in America's favor with the great naval victory at Midway in June 1942 (above). Continued American success in the Pacific illustrated the importance of superior intelligence— achieved by cracking the Japanese navy's message coding system. The human cost of raising the American flag on Japanese-occupied islands from Guadalcanal and the Philippines in 1944 to Iwo Jima (right) and Okinawa in 1945 led U.S. military commanders to warn of huge casualties if a land invasion of Japan proved necessary. Such grim calculations spurred FDR to seek Stalin's commitment of Soviet forces to the Far East once victory had been achieved in Europe. They would also frame Harry Truman's decision to drop the atomic bomb in August 1945.

The 1944 Election

By November 1944 FDR was visibly frail as he and Eleanor hit the campaign trail for reelection (far left). He was not the strong and confident figure whom the poster urged to "stay and finish the job" (left). G.I.s in London and other overseas stations were able to vote and took a keen interest (above). Roosevelt and his new vice president, Harry Truman, won by the narrowest popular vote margin of FDR's four presidential elections, but with a comfortable majority of 432 to 99 in the electoral college.

Realpolitik at Yalta

In failing health, Roosevelt joined Churchill and Stalin at the Soviet Black Sea resort of Yalta in February 1945. Soviet forces had driven the Nazis out of Yugoslavia and penetrated Austria, Hungary, and Czechoslovakia. As the occupying power, the Soviet Union had begun establishing interim Communist governments in Poland, Romania, and Bulgaria. The Red Army was only fifty miles from Berlin while the American forces had been slowed by the German counteroffensive known as the Battle of the Bulge. With so little leverage over Stalin, it was less ill health (or inside treachery, as some FDR-haters would have it) than military realities that led FDR to extract no firmer guarantees over Poland than a vague commitment to free elections sometime. Given that the Nazi invasion of Poland had prompted the British declaration of war, Churchill's acquiescence over that nation's fate is more telling than Roosevelt's failure to dictate terms. Nonetheless, as anti-Communism gathered strength in the U.S. and Soviet repression intensified in the 1940s, a myth of Yalta would be coined by Republicans that pointed accusingly at the State Department and implied betrayal.

Truman's Accession

On the afternoon of April 12, at his "little White House" in Warm Springs, Georgia, Franklin Roosevelt died of a stroke at the age of sixty-three. Weeping crowds lined Connecticut Avenue as the funeral cortege brought his body to the White House prior to burial (opposite). The man who had been president longer than any other was beloved by many and loathed by others, and his death did not heal divisions. A New York taxi driver recalled a passenger gloating, "Thank God, that bastard's dead!" The driver continued: "I didn't think about the fare. I just yanked him from the cab and slugged him!" With his wife Bess and daughter Margaret at his side, the unprepossessing Harry Truman took the oath of office (above). The Democratic Party, like the country, was unsure what to expect of him.

Cold World Order

To signal continuity with FDR's plans and placate liberals, Truman gave Eleanor Roosevelt a key role in the development of the United Nations (opposite). One of her proudest achievements came when the UN adopted the Declaration of Human Rights in 1948, and she remained part of the U.S. delegation until 1953. The UN was largely defined at the San Francisco Conference in June 1945 (above). But failure to agree on an atomic energy control plan in 1946 proved that the UN could not harmonize U.S.–Soviet relations. Fears of Communist expansion in Europe deepened in 1947. First the Truman Doctrine committed the U.S. to defend "free people" against "attempted subjugation," and then the European Recovery Plan (right), called the Marshall Plan after secretary of state General George Marshall, used economic aid to revive Western Europe. The North Atlantic Treaty cemented an anti-Soviet Western alliance (NATO) in April 1949.

·ALL OUR COLOURS TO THE MAST·

1948: Surprise Victory

Few people gave Truman a "toot" of a chance in 1948 (right, at the Democratic Convention). A year after FDR's death, less than a third of the American public backed him in the polls. Republican victories confirmed that inflation and strikes had damaged the party. By passing the Taft-Hartley Act over Truman's veto, however, Republicans won back support for the Democrats from organized labor. White ethnic voters liked Truman's cold war stance, and Jewish voters applauded his support for the new state of Israel. African Americans cheered the recommendations of his liberal Committee on Civil Rights and his order to desegregate the armed forces. The New Deal coalition was rallying behind him, except for the white South. Truman could not appease both Wallace-style liberals and Southern segregationists (below right). Truman tried compromise, but the convention adopted a liberal civil rights plank. Written off in the press right up to election night printing deadlines (left), "Give 'em Hell" Harry had the last laugh on premature headlines.

The South Bolts

Until 1936 the convention rules had required a two-thirds majority for the nominee, which had given the South an effective veto. FDR's attempted 1938 purge, his selection of a non-Southern running mate in 1940, and challenges to seating all-white Deep South delegations by interracial Progressive Democrats at the 1944 convention all pushed the snowball of Southern resentment prior to 1948. Aware that his own actions had angered the Southern bloc, Truman went to the Philadelphia convention hoping to secure a moderate civil rights plank that would keep Deep South delegates like Strom Thurmond of South Carolina (above, looming on the right) inside the party. From the floor, however, young Minneapolis mayor Hubert Humphrey gave an impassioned speech. To cheers and jeers he declared, "The time has arrived in America for the Democratic Party to get out of the shadow of states' rights and walk forthrightly into the bright sunshine of human rights!" When the convention adopted a more liberal position, the Mississippi and Alabama delegations left in fury (right).

The Dixiecrats Fail

After storming out of the Philadelphia convention, Deep South delegates reconvened in Birmingham, Alabama, to select a presidential ticket for their new States' Rights Party. While excited college students waved the Confederate flag (right), they chose Governor Strom Thurmond of South Carolina, with Governor Fielding Wright of Mississippi as his running mate. Hopes of an inconclusive electoral college result that would force the election into the House of Representatives failed. Although thirty-nine Thurmond electors ran and won as official Democratic candidates— in Alabama, Louisiana, Mississippi, and South Carolina—elsewhere, as independents, they lost to Truman slates, reflecting Truman's retention of 50 percent of the total Southern vote compared to Thurmond's 23 percent. The split over civil rights opened the way for future Republican victories.

The Hiss Case

In the summer of 1948 the House Un-American Activities Committee heard evidence from senior *Time* editor Whittaker Chambers about his Communist contacts as a party member in the 1930s. He identified the then-president of the Carnegie Endowment for International Peace, Alger Hiss, as having belonged to a Communist cell. Hiss denied knowing Chambers, but the fact that Hiss had been at Yalta and helped to organize the San Francisco Conference fed the suspicion that here possibly was a Communist at the heart of government. Republican congressman Richard Nixon demanded further hearings to establish whether Chambers (right, arms folded) or Hiss (left, handcuffed to a fellow prisoner) was lying. After a hung jury failed to convict Hiss of perjury in 1948, he was tried for a second time in 1949. In the interim, however, Truman was forced to confirm that the Soviet Union had successfully exploded an atomic bomb (below left), a result many attributed to espionage. In the charged atmosphere of the times, a second grand jury found Hiss guilty in January 1950, and he was sentenced to five years. By acting as character witnesses for Hiss, prominent Democrats Dean Acheson and Adlai Stevenson were smeared by association.

The Red Scare

Hungry for publicity, HUAC investigated Communist infiltration of Hollywood in 1947. Of the nineteen suspects summoned before the committee, ten, including scriptwriter Dalton Trumbo (left), cited the First Amendment as not requiring them to answer questions about their personal beliefs. Liberal stars including Humphrey Bogart, Lauren Bacall, and Danny Kaye flew to Washington to offer support (right). The so-called Hollywood Ten were found guilty of contempt and eventually jailed in 1950. Once released, they could find no further work in Hollywood, due to the blacklist, as had earlier been the fate of the great singer Paul Robeson (above). His income from performances shrank from over $100,000 in 1947 to barely $2,000 in 1950. Seeing the success of HUAC's tactics, Wisconsin Senator Joseph McCarthy (above left) insisted in February 1950 that there were Communists in the State Department, and Dean Acheson was doing nothing about it. The Korean War, on top of other Communist advances, fueled the perception that treachery was endangering the nation, and McCarthy's accusations stained American life for four more years.

Truman Fires MacArthur

On April 11, 1951, President Truman sacked General Douglas MacArthur (opposite). A hero of two world wars, MacArthur had demonstrated battlefield brilliance by reversing North Korean gains through his daring landings at Inchon. Lionized at home, he wanted to respond to Chinese support for North Korea by expanding the war and even using nuclear weapons. Truman, on the other hand, wanted an armistice that would formalize Korean partition at the 38th Parallel. Openly insubordinate, MacArthur sabotaged negotiations until Truman fired him. But by failing to divulge MacArthur's misconduct, Truman allowed himself to be painted as the gulity party by rumors that percolated into protest (above), and by Republicans like Nixon (right, clutching telegrams he has received demanding Truman's impeachment).

1952: Not So Gladly for Adlai

The election was likely to be a dirty campaign with Republican Red Scare tactics and charges of corruption in the air. To the delight of local backers (right), euphoric Democrats on the third ballot chose Illinois governor Adlai Stevenson (left, campaigning in New England). He had won his 1948 gubernatorial race by the largest plurality in state history and earned praise from both business and organized labor for his anticorruption policies. Stevenson's wit and eloquence, it was hoped, would expose the inadequacies of "Red-baiting," and with Alabama senator John Sparkman on the ticket, the Solid South might return. Stevenson had plenty of youthful support (below left), but it was not enough, and the Eisenhower-Nixon ticket won comfortably.

The Party of Labor

Organized labor was a key Democratic constituency by the 1950s, and Southern conservative misgivings about the party in the late 1940s had largely confirmed labor's allegiance. Purged of Communist unions, the CIO gave its full weight (above, in convention) to the Democrats in 1952.

With collective bargaining securing tangible benefits, the CIO came to appreciate the "bread-and-butter" unionism of the AFL. Hands joined, AFL's George Meany (opposite, on the left) and CIO's Walter Reuther salute their 1955 merger.

Adlai Tries Again

Despite stirrings from new contenders like Senator John F. Kennedy of Massachusetts and new-style Southerners Lyndon Johnson of Texas and Estes Kefauver of Tennessee, the nominee remained Adlai Stevenson in 1956. Keen not to alienate Southern support by championing civil rights, Stevenson campaigned instead on a progressive foreign policy, suggesting that the time had come to end the draft and to reduce international tensions by halting nuclear testing. Despite some campaign success (right), public concern over the Suez Canal crisis favored Eisenhower, and support for Stevenson in the election shrank to a belt of just seven Southern states.

The Southern Freedom Struggle

In the mid-1950s renewed demands for racial justice presented the Democratic Party with a fresh challenge. In Montgomery the young Martin Luther King Jr. (above) was arrested for leading a yearlong boycott of the segregated bus system. The U.S. Supreme Court ordered the desegregation of Montgomery buses in December 1956. Such court orders, beginning with the school desegregation cases in 1954, faced intransigent—and often violent—Southern resistance. In 1957 Democratic governor Orval Faubus's refusal to protect nine black students authorized to attend Little Rock's Central High School forced Eisenhower to deploy federal troops (right). A Democratic president would have partisan as well as moral dilemmas.

The 1960 Nomination Race

At the start of the race, party regulars favored
Hubert Humphrey (above), an eloquent and
consistent champion of liberal values and labor
interests. Equally impressive was Senate Majority
Leader Lyndon Johnson (right), whose biggest
asset—being a Southerner—was simultaneously
his biggest weakness. And then there was John F.
Kennedy—with Stevenson's wit, Johnson's love of
politicking, Humphrey's eloquence, his father's
money, and his own unequaled style. By beating
Humphrey in the West Virginia primary (left),
Kennedy proved that his Catholicism was not an
insurmountable barrier and that he had a team
that could win. At the convention, the first
ballot saw him home, and Johnson accepted
second place on the ticket.

Debates and Deals

The closely fought 1960 contest seemed to turn on two incidents. The first was a campaign innovation: the radio-television debate. In the critical first debate (above), those who tuned in on the radio felt that Nixon won. But the TV audience preferred the tanned, handsome Kennedy to the sweaty, swarthy Nixon and adjudged Kennedy the winner. The second incident involved Kennedy's younger brother Bobby. After one of their frequent consultations (right), JFK phoned Martin Luther King's wife Coretta to express concern at her husband's imprisonment in Georgia for civil rights activities, while Bobby rang Georgia Democratic insiders to help spring King from jail. After the election, Eisenhower said that the result hinged on a couple of phone calls that Nixon refused to make.

Kennedy Fever

The closeness of the election could not disguise the fact that Kennedy had tapped a new excitement in the party and the public. At forty-three, the youngest man ever elected to the office, Kennedy's youth and apparent vigor had an appeal not seen since the early years of FDR. Like Roosevelt, the public persona concealed private pain—from the back injury that required a corset and from the drugs that controlled his Addison's disease. In a mass media election, style was everything, and the Kennedy style inspired Democrats.

Chapter Six

Broken Dreams

1960—1980

Broken Dreams
1960–1980

THE KENNEDY-JOHNSON TICKET WON THE closest election since 1888 with a winning margin of just 118,574 votes out of 68 million cast. Yet the absence of a clear popular mandate was obscured on a snowy February Inauguration Day by the style JFK brought to the office. With the elegant and beautiful Jacqueline beside him, he dazzled his audience with an appeal to ideals. "Let every nation know," he proclaimed, "whether it wishes us well or ill, that we shall pay any price, bear any burden, meet any hardship, support any friend, oppose any foe, to assure the survival and success of liberty." JFK exuded confidence.

Describing himself as an "idealist without illusions," Kennedy wanted tough, pragmatic figures in his cabinet. He appointed men like Defense Secretary Robert McNamara, who had turned around the fortunes of the Ford Motor Company, or his national security adviser McGeorge Bundy, whom Kennedy dryly observed was "the second smartest man I know." He also rewarded his younger brother and loyal campaign aide, Bobby Kennedy, by making him attorney general, the nation's top legal officer. He quipped to reporters that he could not "see the harm in Bobby getting a little experience before he goes into law practice." With older rival Adlai Stevenson exiled to the United Nations and defeated challenger Lyndon Johnson sulking in the vice presidential chair and exchanging scowls with his nemesis Bobby Kennedy, the "best and the brightest" set out to build Camelot.

Reality, however, intruded rapidly. Kennedy had campaigned against the lethargy of the Eisenhower administration. Now he discovered not only that the "missile gap" he had alleged did not exist, but that plans to topple Castro's new Communist regime in Cuba were well advanced. Assured that a scheme to land Cuban rebels at the Bay of Pigs was feasible, he allowed it to go ahead in April 1961. The result was a fiasco that made the U.S. look "like fools to our friends, rascals to our enemies, and incompetents to the rest." A confrontational summit meeting regarding Berlin with Soviet premier Khrushchev followed. The Berlin Wall was suddenly constructed by the East Germans, and Khrushchev resumed atmospheric nuclear testing in the autumn of 1961. The burden and the price Kennedy had alluded to at the start of the year was rising.

With daughter Caroline on election day 1960, John F. Kennedy looked proudly and confidently forward.

Previous pages: JFK at his desk while Attorney General Robert Kennedy stands at the Oval Office window, April 1962.

Defense Secretary Robert McNamara, a master of systems analysis for Ford, was among the "best and the brightest" recruited from business and academe in 1961.

First Lady Jacqueline Bouvier Kennedy brought glamour and style to the White House.

Domestically, the most disturbing question was the growing civil rights protests against segregation in the South. Having helped Southern Senate colleagues limit the scope of the 1957 Civil Rights Act, Kennedy's position was that progress could come from vigorous executive action rather than new legislation. He singled out segregation in federal housing as an injustice that could be swept away with "a stroke of a pen." As months passed without a housing desegregation order, black leaders orchestrated a "send a pen to Jack" campaign.

With foreign policy his priority, Kennedy was deeply concerned when white supremacists embarrassed the nation by attacking buses and interracial passengers taking part in a Freedom Ride in the summer of 1961. The Supreme Court had ruled against segregated interstate buses and terminals, and the Freedom Ride was to test Southern compliance, or rather, defiance. As head of the Justice Department, Bobby Kennedy was primarily responsible for dealing with the crisis. He gave limited federal protection (U.S. marshals rather than troops) and pressed the Interstate Commerce Commission to issue guidelines that would bite hard on Southern business if defied. Neither Kennedy brother liked civil rights leader Martin Luther King's utopian approach to politics.

Caution on civil rights reflected Kennedy's concern not to antagonize powerful Southern politicians on the Hill who occupied important committee positions such as Appropriations and Defense. Under increasing pressure from civil rights groups, he forced the integration of the University of Mississippi, despite mob action, in 1962. After the shocking scenes of Alabama police attacking protesters in 1963, he submitted civil rights legislation. To demonstrate the national consensus for racial reform, a mass March on Washington was held on August 28, 1963. Martin Luther King delivered his famous "I Have a Dream" speech, which added to the momentum for federal action. But even before Kennedy seemed to be coming down on the side of black demands, the Southern caucus blocked increased federal aid to education, health insurance for the aged, and other social welfare and foreign aid initiatives. They appropriated more money than Kennedy requested for defense and backed a space program to land a man on the moon: Both would send federal tax dollars southward. As Kennedy planned his reelection campaign, he knew he would have to placate the party's Southern wing somehow.

Kennedy's leadership skills grew considerably in office, particularly with the scary Cuban Missile Crisis of October 1962. Soviet missile installations were detected under construction in Cuba, and Kennedy announced a naval blockade of the island on October 22. When Soviet vessels threatened to run the blockade, a catastrophic nuclear exchange loomed. Khrushchev, however, drew back, offering to withdraw the missiles in return for a U.S. pledge not to invade Cuba. Kennedy responded favorably to this, leaving a second demand for the removal of U.S. missiles from Turkey to one side. In the aftermath of this "eyeball-to-eyeball" confrontation, U.S.–Soviet relations improved. A hot line was installed between the White House and Kremlin, obsolete U.S. missiles were withdrawn from Turkey, and negotiations began for a nuclear test ban treaty. Disarmament remained remote, but as Kennedy said, quoting a Chinese proverb: "A journey of a thousand miles begins with one step."

Apart from the Cuban situation that ensnared JFK, the Eisenhower administration had handed over a degenerating crisis in the former French colony of Indochina, which "Quiet American" operatives had been monitoring throughout the 1950s. Communist insurgency threatened pro-Western regimes in Laos and South Vietnam. Diplomacy seemed to contain the problem in Laos, but the unpopular regime of Ngo Dinh Diem appeared to be losing control in South Vietnam, despite assistance from U.S. military advisers. When Kennedy took office, there were 2,000 advisers in Vietnam, and in October 1963 the U.S. ambassador, Henry Cabot Lodge, effectively gave local generals the green light for a coup against Diem. Diem was violently overthrown, but South Vietnam remained deeply unstable. By the end of the year, in spite of Kennedy's assurances that he expected the U.S. to be out of Vietnam in two years, 16,000 American advisers were there to stop this domino from falling.

At 1:34 P.M. EST, November 22, 1963, Americans across the country began to experience what psychologists call "flashbulb memory," the freeze-framing of an exceptionally emotional event down to the last detail. Many still remember precisely where they were and what they were doing when they heard that President Kennedy had been shot in Dallas. It equaled the shock of Pearl Harbor in 1941 and has since been matched only by the events of September 11, 2001.

The trauma of the young president's sudden death, the disbelief at the murder of the accused assassin, Lee Harvey Oswald, captured on television, and the poignancy of the state funeral with Kennedy's son saluting his father's casket combined unbearably. Vice President Johnson took the oath of office on the plane that took Kennedy's body back to Washington. Rough-hewn and coarse, where Kennedy was smooth and suave, Lyndon Baines Johnson nonetheless matched his predecessor in

James Meredith became the first black student at the University of Mississippi in the fall of 1962, under Kennedy's auspices.

The grim headlines that shocked the nation and the world on November 22, 1963.

political ambition and arguably surpassed him in his mastery of legislative politics. In 1951 he had become the youngest-ever Senate minority leader in Democratic Party history. Three years later he became the majority leader and demonstrated his manipulative gifts for ensuring a bill's passage by shepherding nearly 1,300 bills through the Senate by horse-trading, backroom, or more accurately, phone calls, deals, and intense personal lobbying that insiders called the "Johnson treatment." Observers likened the treatment to hypnosis and claimed that it sometimes "rendered the target stunned and helpless." Spending hours on the phone each day, Johnson loved gossip and was quite willing to threaten embarrassment to get his way. Once asked if a senator would vote as instructed, LBJ replied, "I find that once you have a man by the balls, he tends to follow your lead."

Amid national grief, Johnson determined to pass Kennedy's stymied legislative program and to create a record in domestic policy to match that of his idol, FDR. His priorities, according to his first State of the Union address, were the Kennedy tax cut, the civil rights bill, and an "unconditional war on poverty in America." This list was bolder and less oriented to foreign policy than Kennedy's had been. It also marked an apotheosis of the New Deal goal of using government to help people.

The tax cut boosted consumer demand and the economy at a time when inflation was relatively low, but in later years Democrats were accused of "overheating" the economy through federal spending programs and allowing inflation to get out of control. Passage of the 1964 Civil Rights Act reflected Johnson's belief that his native South had been held back for too long by a racial order that wasted human lives. Further, the stagnant racial order ensured a political climate in which liberals like himself were continuously threatened by the conservative appeal of white supremacy. He told his one-time mentor, Senator Richard Russell of Georgia, who had orchestrated resistance to civil rights legislation, to accept defeat. With Hubert Humphrey coordinating strategy on the Hill, LBJ broke Southern resistance and passed the bill. It swept away segregation in public accommodation, launched policies to end job discrimination due to race, religion, national origin, or sex, gave teeth at last to the Supreme Court's long-standing order to desegregate schools, and made it harder to use literacy tests to deny voting rights.

By the time of the 1964 Democratic National Convention in Atlantic City, Lyndon Johnson seemed unchallenged for the nomination due to his success in enacting the fallen Kennedy's legacy. He himself feared

President Lyndon Johnson spent hours politicking on the phone. His powers of persuasion were legendary on Capitol Hill.

that there might be some attempt to draft Bobby Kennedy after delegates watched an emotional tribute to his brother. More realistically, Johnson feared that the scale of opposition to his civil rights policy among white Southerners might grow unless care was taken at the convention. He was keenly aware of an ongoing effort to organize black voters in Mississippi, called "Freedom Summer." The campaign had cost three lives (one black Mississippian and two white New York volunteers), victims of white supremacists in early August, and there were plans to challenge the seating of the all-white, regular Mississippi delegation. An interracial Mississippi Freedom Democratic Party applied to be seated at the convention and presented evidence of the brutality used to exclude them from regular Democratic politics in the Magnolia State.

Despite his commitment to racial reform, Johnson alienated the MFDP. He called a snap press conference to deflect media attention from Fannie Lou Hamer's dramatic testimony and warned Hubert Humphrey that if a deal was not brokered, Humphrey could forget the vice presidential nomination. The deal—to require the regulars to swear loyalty to the party platform and ticket, to award the MFDP two delegates at large, and to appoint a commission to ensure racial inclusiveness at future conventions—was soured by LBJ's high-handed tactics. "We didn't come all this way for no two seats," declared Hamer. Rounding on figures like King, who argued that the compromise had political advantages, student leader Bob Moses said, "We're not here to bring politics to our morality, but to bring morality to our politics."

The MFDP rejection proved a turning point for both the civil rights movement and the Democratic Party. Despite Johnson following up on his reelection with a swath of positive antipoverty measures that would address African American needs and the powerful Voting Rights Act, which promised to reenfranchise Southern blacks, militants dismissed liberal Democrats as part of an irredeemable establishment. After 1966 they urged political separatism via third parties to achieve Black Power. Johnson himself was gloomily sanguine about the consequences of the Voting Rights Act, saying that he had probably ended Democratic control of the South for at least a generation.

Within days of Johnson signing the Voting Rights Act into law, the Los Angeles district of Watts erupted into violent racial disturbances that left thirty-five people dead. When this pattern of urban disorder proliferated across major cities in the next few years, it fueled a white backlash that questioned the legitimacy of black demands and the effectiveness of Democratic politicians. Martin Luther King

Wilbur D. Mills, chairman of the House budget committee, played a pivotal role in approving LBJ's raft of social welfare programs, notably Medicare.

Chicago boss, Mayor Richard J. Daley, typified the Democratic Party establishment going into the 1960s and became a prime target for youthful dissenters.

illustrated the depths of this problem by campaigning in Mayor Richard Daley's Chicago in 1966. The outrage of white home owners against interracial "open housing" marches that summer illustrated that tackling institutional racism nationwide would be even more difficult than dismantling Southern segregation had been. It also showed that having lost some Southern support due to racial liberalism, the Democrats might jeopardize their traditional white working-class vote in key industrial states by identifying too closely with African American demands.

Elected by a landslide against Republican Barry Goldwater in 1964, LBJ demanded that his advisers take advantage of Democratic majorities in both the House and Senate. "Every day I'm in office," he told aides, "I'm going to lose votes. I'm going to alienate somebody.… We've got to get this legislation fast." Fulfilling a pledge that dated back to Harry Truman's Fair Deal, Congress established the Medicare/Medicaid programs. Johnson enacted federal aid for education and with echoes of the New Deal's TVA passed the Appalachian Development Act. Little debated in the flood of legislation, but of huge consequence, Congress passed the 1965 Immigration Act, which abolished the quotas that had favored Nordic immigration since the 1920s. It set a ceiling of 120,000 immigrants from inside the Western Hemisphere and 170,000 from outside, and excluded family members of current residents from these limits. Soon, a fresh wave of immigration of Hispanics and Asians was set to remake American society in the same way as Irish and Eastern European immigrants had done in the nineteenth century.

From the foot of the Statue of Liberty in New York Harbor, President Johnson speaks at the signing of the 1965 Immigration Act, which permitted a new wave of immigration.

Johnson had wanted his administration to be remembered for progressive legislation that made America into the "Great Society," but as his term neared its end, the one topic associated with it was Vietnam. Johnson was similar to Harry Truman in his yearning for simplicity in foreign relations. He did not have Kennedy's cosmopolitan view of the world. When asked why he had not turned to the Organization of American States to defuse a crisis in the Caribbean, he had snapped, "The OAS couldn't pour piss out of a boot, even if the instructions were written on the heel." Having seen Truman enveloped by a Red Scare because of setbacks in China and Korea, Johnson was determined to prove that he was tough enough to contain Communism in Vietnam.

An alleged attack on U.S. vessels in the Gulf of Tonkin in August 1964 prompted Congress to grant the president wide powers to commit troops. By 1968 this permitted Johnson to send over half a million Americans to fight in Vietnam and to extend operations to Laos without seeking congressional approval. As military commanders demanded more bombing raids and more troops to achieve an elusive victory, Johnson went along with them, mesmerized by the promise of light at the end of the tunnel. Domestic opposition to the war mounted as television coverage brought the horrors of the conflict into people's homes.

The war caused grave divisions across society, with many wondering how they could support a war that set children alight with chemical weapons, made young Americans capable of massacring civilians as at My Lai, and aligned their government with a regime that summarily executed opponents in the street. By 1968 demands for a bombing halt and peace negotiations were growing so acute that rivals such as Senator Eugene McCarthy of Minnesota and Robert Kennedy, now senator for New York, felt they could challenge Johnson for the 1968 nomination. Despondent and with a sense of his failing health, Johnson announced on March 31 that he would not seek the nomination. Four days later Martin Luther King, an outspoken opponent of the war, was killed in Memphis. His murder triggered a wave of serious race riots, notably in Washington itself. Two months later shocked Democrats saw RFK accept his victory over Eugene McCarthy in the California primary before being felled by assassin Sirhan Sirhan. By the time of the national convention in August, the gulf between the old guard, symbolized by Chicago's mayor Richard Daley inside the convention, and the youthful antiwar protesters outside was all too evident as Daley's police beat up demonstrators in front of a huge live television audience.

The defeat of Hubert Humphrey by Richard Nixon in November ended a dispiriting year that left the Democrats shell-shocked and divided. The party went into the 1972 campaign still haunted by its efforts to woo young and minority constituencies who were more fully represented at the Miami convention than ever before. With 15 percent of delegates to the convention black, Representative Shirley Chisholm of New York became the first African American to seek the Democratic presidential nomination. In 1968 only 3 percent of delegates had been under thirty years of age; four years later, at the convention that nominated George McGovern and urged liberalization of marijuana laws, they constituted 23 percent. On election day Nixon won every state but Massachusetts.

Central to the party's future was the changing character of Southern politics since the Voting Rights Act of 1965 enabled African Americans to register in large numbers for the first time in generations. In some cases, established political figures adapted to the new system and courted

Burning the American flag came to symbolize student opposition to the Vietnam War and reflected a larger questioning of old truths.

George McGovern with running mate Thomas Eagleton, who was replaced by Sargent Shriver during the 1972 campaign. The election result was one of the worst ever for the Democrats

the black vote with the same mixture of favors and promises that they had previously extended to whites alone. In a few black majority districts, it became prudent for the Democratic Party to select black candidates for office, but more generally it was felt that African Americans had to be exceptional figures to have crossover appeal. By the mid-1970s it was unclear whether newcomers like Senators Sam Nunn of Georgia and Dale Bumpers of Arkansas would prove as important to the party as older-style Southern politicians like Senator John Sparkman of Alabama.

In the event, it was a peanut farmer from Plains, Georgia, James Earl Carter, who profited from popular revulsion at the Watergate scandals to secure an unexpected Democratic victory in the 1976 presidential election. Little known outside his home state before the primaries, he was preferred by Democrats over Walter Mondale because he seemed to represent a fresh start, untainted by Washington. Viewed as an honest man, he seemed to restore the New Deal coalition of a solid South and key industrial states. He did not, however, reverse the continuing fall in voter turnout (54.4 percent in 1976). This suggested that political parties were losing their hold on the public imagination. "Don't Vote," a bumper sticker declared, "It Only Encourages Them."

Carter's malaise: Foreign weakness spilled over into domestic crisis in 1979, when Iranian oil sanctions produced long lines at gas stations.

Carter had appealed to minorities and appointed many African Americans, Hispanics, and women to high office. Black civil rights leader Andrew Young became UN ambassador and helped improve relations with Africa. Perhaps Carter's greatest achievement, however, was securing the 1978 Camp David Accords that made peace between Egypt and Israel. Here again was another Southern Democrat who unexpectedly found himself dealing with international problems. Damning his chances of reelection, however, was a weak economy that combined both unemployment and inflation and a growing impression that the idealistic president was unable to protect American interests.

When Iranian Islamic militants overthrew the shah in 1979, they also decided to target his chief foreign sponsor, the United States. They drove up oil prices, and then in November the U.S. Embassy was stormed and dozens of Americans were taken hostage. Carter seemed impotent, an impression deepened by the simultaneous Soviet invasion of Afghanistan. Desperate to regain public confidence, Carter approved a commando-style raid to free the hostages in April 1980. It ended in disaster, and the president, after a bitter nomination fight with Senator Ted Kennedy, faced an uphill struggle against the buoyant Republican nominee, Ronald Reagan, in November.

The Kennedy Style

Fulfilling a lifetime's ambition through his son, proud father Joseph P. Kennedy stands beside President John F. Kennedy on January 21, 1961 (above). A glittering spectacle, the inaugural ceremonies illustrated the Kennedy style. Hardheaded political calculation, exemplified by JFK's tactical selection of Texan Lyndon Johnson as his running mate, might require uncomfortable alliances. But in the new media age, it also required a sharply managed image, and the Kennedy administration would cultivate an air of youthful easy elegance, embodied in the exquisitely dressed figure of Jackie and the witty repartee of JFK himself. If Jackie could make a Southern boy like LBJ look good and feel good in a tuxedo (right), she would do wonders for the administration's public presentation.

JFK and Cuba: Act I—The Bay of Pigs

Fidel Castro's 1959 Cuban Revolution (poster, left) overthrew the corrupt, but American-friendly, Batista regime. By the time of the 1960 presidential election, the island's bearded left-wing leader had alarmed the U.S. He had forged close ties with Nikita Khrushchev's Soviet Union (right) and nationalized American-owned companies. While president-elect, JFK was informed of plans for an invasion of Cuba. Assured by the CIA that U.S. involvement would be covert, he approved what became known as the Bay of Pigs fiasco, a disastrous invasion in April 1961 that left Cuban exiles angry and Castro stronger. The plot also diminished JFK's international standing in the run-up to the Vienna Summit (below). There, Khrushchev berated Kennedy so harshly over Berlin that the new president returned home depressed but determined. He would deal with Castro and show Khrushchev that he was no lightweight.

Freedom Now!

In May 1961 protesters boarded buses to
test compliance with a Supreme Court order
desegregating Southern bus terminals. In Alabama
white supremacists attacked these Freedom Riders
and sympathetic reporters (opposite). To contain
an embarrassing spectacle, Attorney General
Robert Kennedy brokered a deal. Hostile state
authorities agreed to have National Guardsmen
protect the protesters (above), but were allowed to
arrest them when they reached their destination in
Mississippi. RFK and Justice Department colleague
Byron White (right) assumed the protesters would
file bail, leaving their cases to be settled in the
hush of the courts, while Interstate Commerce
Commission rules could be drafted to ensure bus
terminal desegregation. However, the Freedom
Riders chose jail, ensuring fresh headlines and
more worries for RFK.

JFK and Cuba: Act II—The Missile Crisis

U-2 spy plane reconnaissance flights over Cuba confirmed in October 1962 that Soviet intermediate-range ballistic missile sites were under construction in Cuba. This alarmingly escalated the tensions that had continued since the failed Bay of Pigs invasion the previous year. The new missiles were offensive rather than defensive weapons and could deliver a nuclear strike against most American cities. Some advisers urged immediate air strikes before the missiles became fully operational. Others, notably Robert Kennedy, proposed a naval blockade of Cuba. The president informed the nation of the increased threat of nuclear war via television on October 22 (above) and announced the blockade. Any weapon fired from Cuba, he declared, would be regarded "as an attack by the Soviet Union on the United States," which would require a "full retaliatory response." At the same time, UN ambassador Adlai Stevenson (right) rallied support against the Soviet threat.

Eyeball to Eyeball

The American naval blockade of Cuba carried grave risks. As it became clear that Soviet vessels were approaching the exclusion area, millions held their breath. If the Soviets refused to stop and came under attack from U.S. warships, this might easily escalate to full-scale nuclear war. Kennedy judged correctly that his Soviet counterpart, Khrushchev, was prepared to back down, provided he could do so without intolerable loss of face. He sensed that in the Kremlin, as in the White House, there were hawks as well as doves, especially when he received two very different messages from Khrushchev, one bellicose and the other conciliatory in tone. Encouraged by Bobby, who was at his side throughout the crisis, Kennedy crucially chose to ignore the former and instead responded positively to the latter. His coolness and unwillingness either to buckle or lash out under such pressure earned Kennedy great respect. Khrushchev ordered the withdrawal of the missiles. American promises to respect Cuban independence seemed a modest concession by comparison, and the later withdrawal of aging U.S. missiles from Turkey was not publicly linked to the deal at the time. The general impression was that it was Khrushchev who blinked.

Man of the World

In the summer of 1963 President Kennedy visited Europe again. Underlining the new élan with which he strode the world stage was his visit to West Berlin, which Khrushchev had tried to scare him into yielding in 1961. The exodus of skilled workers from East Berlin had led the East German government to construct the infamous Berlin Wall. Before this symbol of Communism's failure, Kennedy delivered one of his most famous speeches (above). He promised to defend West Berlin, and despite some ambiguity in the original German, his declaration of solidarity—"*Ich bin ein Berliner*" ("I am a Berliner")—was seen as a rhetorical masterstroke, one that later presidents would seek to emulate. Another sign of renewed confidence was a triumphant visit to Ireland, where JFK delighted the crowds (right). During the 1960 election there had been fears that his Irish Catholic background would damage his candidacy just as it had sunk Al Smith's in 1928. It had not proved decisive, and now Kennedy was confident enough to rejoice in his ethnic ties. The consensus was that he had matured in office, developing a more sophisticated vision of international affairs. Negotiations with the Soviet Union over disarmament had yielded a nuclear test ban treaty, and instead of using his 1950s vocabulary of missile gaps and peace through strength, the president now spoke of the need for coexistence.

King's 1963 March on Washington

Beforehand, the Democratic Party leadership was skeptical about the merits of the mass interracial rally on the Mall for "Jobs and Freedom" (right). A rally was better than the angry protest march that militants had originally urged, of course, but President Kennedy, with his civil rights bill before Congress, felt the event might still alienate wavering supporters, especially if the day degenerated into violent clashes. On August 28, however, the peaceful gathering of nearly a quarter of a million people offered the hope that Americans of all races might come together to share their nation's promise of freedom. The day's final speaker, Dr. Martin Luther King Jr. (above), movingly captured that hope in his "I Have a Dream" speech. The famous "Dream" section was not part of King's prepared text, but was included extemporaneously because anxious organizers had hurried previous speakers so much that the day was running ahead of schedule. Afterward, a mightily relieved President Kennedy congratulated King at a White House reception.

White Resistance and Murder

The battle for racial equality reached a crisis in 1963. Politicians like Governor George Wallace of Alabama (left) bolstered their local position by symbolic stands of defiance. Wallace literally blocked the path of federal officials trying to ensure the court-ordered enrollment of black students at the University of Alabama. Other symbols of bigotry, however, were less successful. In Birmingham, Alabama, the notorious police commissioner Eugene "Bull" Connor (below left) ended the year rejected by the voters. He had become an embarrassing byword for crass police methods by his use of dogs and fire hoses against children during the spring 1963 demonstrations. Even more grim was the September bomb attack on the Sixteenth Street Baptist Church in Birmingham, which killed four black girls attending Sunday school. To their bereaved families, the sympathies of national Democrats, including the president, seemed less substantial than the shocking callousness of local politicians, who could not even bring themselves to attend the funerals (right).

Like Movie Stars

Fascination with the First Family reached a new intensity during the Kennedy years, not least because America's youthful president had such a photogenic family. The administration made available images of the president that reinforced the impression of the relaxed and loving father (above): a man confident enough to take time to enjoy his weekends at Hyannisport with daughter Caroline, son John Jr. ("John John"), and assorted dogs and puppies. Other images of JFK and Jackie captured the millionaire lifestyle that enabled them, for example, to enjoy the America's Cup races from the comfort and vantage point of his father's yacht (right). These were equally important in defining the Kennedy image. Their domesticity might make the Kennedys seem like everyday Americans, but their glamour made everyday Americans dream of living like them.

Prelude to Tragedy

President Kennedy flew to Dallas on November 22, 1963 (left), to consolidate and expand Democratic support in key states like Texas ahead of his 1964 reelection bid. It was supposed to be just a standard campaign stop. A proven crowd-puller, Jackie Kennedy accompanied her husband, as did the vice president and former senator for Texas, Lyndon Johnson (with Lady Bird in the background). The president looked healthy and happy. The First Lady accepted flowers, and in an open limousine with Governor John Connally and his wife, JFK and Jackie led the motorcade into downtown Dallas, waving to applauding crowds (above). Sniper fire rang out a few moments later, killing the president and seriously wounding Governor Connally.

United in Grief

In the quiet of a train car, New York commuters read of the assassination (above). Vice President Johnson was sworn in as president at the earliest opportunity, which proved to be aboard Air Force One (right, flanked by his wife and Mrs. Kennedy) as the slain president's body was flown back to Washington. For days the TV networks gave themselves over to news of the president's assassination, that of his apparent killer, Oswald, and the president's funeral a few days later. There was a huge outpouring of sympathy for the president's family (opposite), who bore themselves with unforgettable dignity throughout the ordeal.

1964: All the Way with LBJ

To the delight of liberal stalwarts like Hubert Humphrey, President Johnson added to the legislative achievements of the New Deal. After the longest debate in congressional history, Humphrey (above) was able to signal that reformers had the votes they needed to secure passage of a comprehensive civil rights act in the summer of 1964. It was therefore as a liberal rather than a Southerner that Johnson (with daughter Lynda, right) accepted the Democratic nomination for reelection in 1964. His stance on civil rights would gift the Deep South states to his Republican opponent, Barry Goldwater, but he would sweep the rest of the nation.

"We Shall Overcome"

The civil rights movement in 1965 seemed the standard-bearer for the nation's ideals (opposite). Through a nonviolent campaign that climaxed in a mass march from Selma to Montgomery, Alabama, Martin Luther King (right, with his wife, Coretta) rallied most Americans to support passage of the Voting Rights Act. President Johnson told Congress that the black struggle was every American's and declared, "We shall overcome." Within days of his signing the act, however, violent disturbances racked the Watts district of Los Angeles (above), and America's racial divisions deepened.

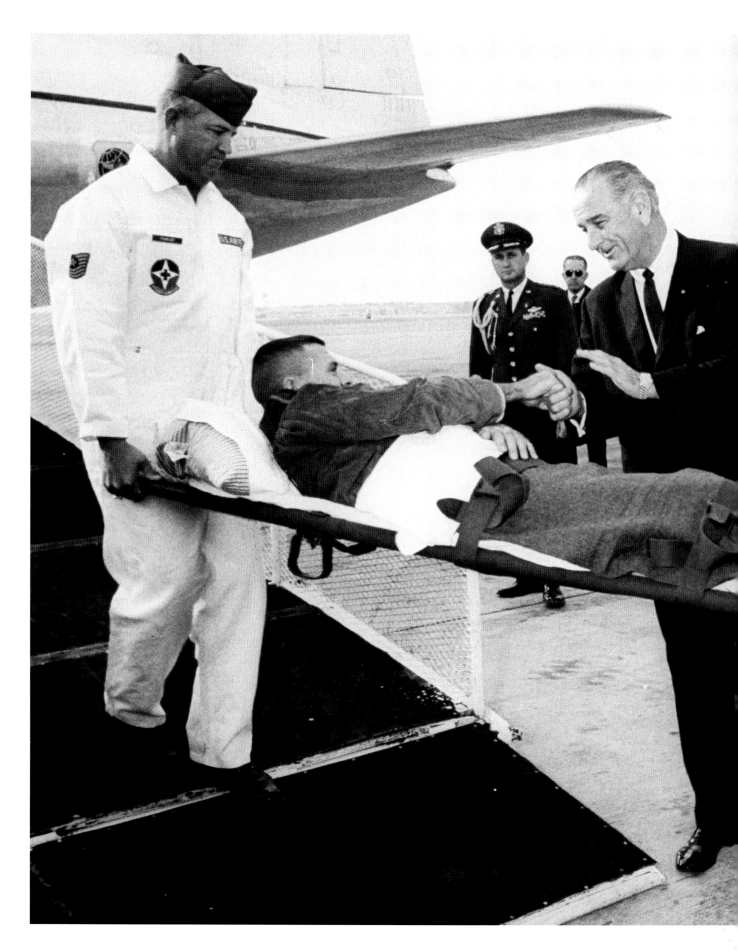

Lyndon's War in Vietnam

In the movie *Goldfinger* (1964), James Bond dealt with international threats easily enough, but as protesters pointed out in 1966 (above), President Johnson was mired in a bloody war against Vietnamese peasants, and there was no end in sight. The product of an era that had seen Democrats lambasted for "being soft on Communism," Lyndon Johnson felt he had to fight to prevent the Vietcong and their North Vietnamese backers from overrunning South Vietnam. Able to escalate U.S. involvement rapidly under powers granted by Congress under the Gulf of Tonkin Resolution of 1964, LBJ had sent 485,000 troops to fight by 1967. Mounting casualties (left) and a lack of progress, however, increasingly damaged the president's standing. The more unpopular the war became, the more it was seen as LBJ's war.

The Deepening Quagmire

The Vietnam War proved the most demoralizing conflict in American history. As a superpower, the United States could deploy the latest military technology—attack helicopters, blanket bombing, and chemical weapons like napalm. Johnson's initial strategy was sustained bombing of North Vietnam, dropping more bombs than American aircraft dropped during World War II. He then tried to pacify the countryside through the rapid deployment of ground troops (left). This intensified the combat experience of inexperienced draftees (average age nineteen) and increased the likelihood of killing civilians caught in sudden firefights. By 1968 the war was consuming Johnson utterly (above), as he struggled for a victory that never came.

Destroying the Dreamer

On April 4, 1968, Dr. Martin Luther King Jr. was shot and killed in Memphis, Tennessee. An outspoken critic of the Vietnam War, King was also organizing a fresh protest campaign to demand action against poverty at the time of his death. A large crowd of mourners follows the casket through the streets of King's hometown of Atlanta, Georgia (top left). King's nonviolent followers struggled to come to terms with their loss (bottom left, Ralph Abernathy and Andrew Young, on the right, touching King's casket). African American communities more generally, however, could not contain their rage. Major cities like Chicago (above) were ablaze in the days following the assassination, and people spoke ominously of their fears that there might now be a second civil war.

The Black Power Movement

Well before Dr. King's death, slow progress toward racial equality had fueled African American disillusionment with white liberals. The Student Nonviolent Coordinating Committee's new chairman, Stokely Carmichael (top left, in front of a photograph of legendary guerrilla fighter Che Guevara), announced in 1966 that, despite its name, SNCC was no longer committed to nonviolence, but to achieving Black Power. Like oppressed people around the world, he

implied, African Americans might need to resort to armed struggle. Carmichael's successor, H. Rap Brown (shown on the poster behind the equally outspoken Eldridge Cleaver of the Black Panther Party, bottom left), deepened this impression by declaring, "Violence is as American as cherry pie." The Black Panthers themselves championed armed

self-defense and became embroiled in a series of armed clashes with local police in Oakland, California, and other cities. With their trademark berets and sunglasses (above), the Panthers became symbols of a new separatism in the black community as they campaigned for the release of their jailed leader, Huey Newton, in 1968.

Give Peace a Chance

With a strong appeal to college youth (above), Senator Eugene McCarthy's 1968 peace campaign came so close to victory in the New Hampshire primary (42 percent to LBJ's 48 percent) that the president astonished the nation by announcing in March 1968 that he would not seek reelection (left). Party regulars responded by switching their support to Vice President Hubert Humphrey, who promised negotiations but no immediate end to the war. The McCarthy challenge continued, but was weakened by the emergence of a new liberal candidate, Robert Kennedy (right). His platform of peace abroad and a renewed war on poverty at home was boosted by a sentimental attachment to his slain brother's memory.

Hope and Despair

In the early summer of 1968 the Kennedy campaign gathered momentum. Gallup polls in April and May showed that Bobby Kennedy was the candidate Democratic voters preferred. He had attended Martin Luther King's funeral in April and was one of the few white politicians to command respect in the black community. People believed that he could reach out to heal an increasingly divided nation. On June 5 a smiling Kennedy, with his wife, Ethel (above), addressed jubilant supporters in a Los Angles hotel after defeating rival Eugene McCarthy in the crucial California primary race. Disappointed at their narrow defeat, just minutes later McCarthy's young supporters (above right) were visibly stunned by the news that Kennedy had been shot and mortally wounded following his victory speech. African Americans in particular gathered along the tracks (below right) to show their respect as a special train carried Kennedy's body from California for burial alongside his brother the president in Arlington Cemetery.

"The Whole World Is Watching"

National party conventions are intended to unite the party behind a common platform and candidates and to rally popular support. But neither aim was fulfilled in 1968. When Democrats gathered in Chicago in August, the nation was still divided over the Vietnam War. Antiwar protesters and student radicals had gathered outside the convention center, and Mayor Daley's police decided to use strong-arm tactics to disperse them. The televised spectacle of tear-gassed and clubbed demonstrators and their chant— "The whole world is watching"— heightened the sense that America's social fabric was in tatters. In a year of mayhem a subsequent official investigation called the incident a "police riot." The very legitimacy of government seemed in doubt.

The Defeat of a Decent Man

With Robert Kennedy's death, support
within the Democratic Party flowed back to
Hubert Humphrey. Ever since he emerged on
the national scene with a dramatic 1948
convention speech, Humphrey had been a
champion of liberal policies and a staunch
supporter of organized labor. While
pandemonium raged outside, inside the
convention his supporters (right) tried to
generate enthusiasm for Humphrey and his
running mate, Edmund Muskie (above).
But despite the promise of responsible
leadership and a lifetime spent in the party's
service, Humphrey could not unite the
bitterly divided party or the nation. In
November he lost narrowly in the popular
vote to Richard Nixon, but more clearly in
the electoral college by 301 to 191 votes.

Space—A New Frontier

The success of the Soviet satellite *Sputnik* in 1957 sparked the space race, but it was John F. Kennedy's 1961 pledge that Americans would land a man on the moon within the decade that defined NASA's mission. By the middle of the decade the program was in full swing. In August 1965 *Gemini V* splashed down safely with Charles "Pete" Conrad Jr. (on the left) and Gordon Cooper aboard. Two months earlier, Ed White on *Gemini IV* had thrilled viewers with the first space walk (above). White perished tragically in a launchpad fire with two other astronauts in 1967.

Liftoff

The *Apollo XI* Moon landings in 1969 occurred shortly after Lyndon Johnson, who had given the space program unstinting support from its inception, had left office. Happily, he and his wife Lady Bird were invited to watch the launch from Cape Kennedy (above). Johnson was never slow to applaud his own achievements, while to his right, Mrs. Johnson clearly shares his pride. On his other side sits a characteristically wooden Spiro T. Agnew, Nixon's eventually disgraced vice president.

The March of Feminism

As the 1970s began, the demand for racial equality had reignited the fight for women's liberation. Underpinned by a structural shift of women into the paid workforce, it was a movement guaranteed to frighten insecure men who had been raised with the hope and the prayer that they would find a compliant mate. The comical flavor of this solitary and hopeless counterfeminist campaign (left) is a measure of feminism's success. With some legal protection in employment thanks to the 1964 Civil Rights Act, but still no Equal Rights Amendment, veteran feminists (above) like Susan B. Anthony II (extreme left), Bella Abzug, and Betty Friedan (in red coat) kept on marching with younger sisters in 1977. They strove to unite women of all backgrounds in the cause.

This Land Is Our Land

After Black Power came Red Power, as spokesmen for nearly 800,000 Native Americans organized themselves to protest ancient grievances and current abuses. Like many blacks, the so-called Indians of America by 1970 saw themselves as a colonized people, trapped in poverty with the highest incidence of alcoholism, tuberculosis, and suicide of any ethnic group in the United States. They would pledge no more allegiance to the American flag. Occupying federal buildings, such as the offices of the Bureau of Indian Affairs in Washington (above), in protest and pursuing their treaty rights through the courts, Native Americans scored notable victories in the 1970s. They regained hunting and fishing rights and secured restitution for lands in Alaska, Maine, and Massachusetts.

Taking the Offensive

As the 1960s ended, student radicalism had become a cliché. From the Students for a Democratic Society's demand for America to live up to its ideals of freedom and justice, it had coarsened into a counterculture that, in the words of Abbie Hoffman (above), believed that the basic "conception of revolution is that it's fun." The counterculture also believed that shock tactics were good tactics, so Hoffman's use of "Old Glory" here was not a bronchial expedient, but a calculated test of patriotic reflexes. When Democrats defended such crudeness in the name of free speech, traditionalists saw them as joining in the insult.

Coming-Out Party

"Gay liberation" emerged publicly from largely closeted homosexual communities in major cities like San Francisco in 1969. A more open attitude to sexuality and a liberalism that celebrated difference and tolerance encouraged gays to equate themselves with women and minorities. Their "natural rights," too, had been wrongly restricted by prejudice. A decade after the Stonewall uprising in New York in 1969 had asserted gay pride, annual gay rights marches (above) saw homosexuals and transvestites proudly flaunt their departure from old models of masculinity. As more traditional citizens rallied to the Republicans in the coming decades, a relatively affluent and articulate gay community would expect the Democratic Party to defend their rights.

The Road to Defeat

A would-be assassin cut short George Wallace's presidential aspirations (right) in May 1972 with a bullet that left him paralyzed from the waist down. By removing his potential to siphon off enough conservative votes from Richard Nixon, the Alabama Dixiecrat's forced withdrawal ended the likelihood of a Democratic victory. The 1972 convention seemed dominated by minority activists. It was the first held under new rules that required state delegations to include representative numbers of women, youth, and minorities. The changes sidelined traditional supporters such as Mayor Daley of Chicago, who was denied a seat. Presidential candidate George McGovern (above left) seemingly owed his nomination to charismatic minority figures like Jesse Jackson (below left), whose style alarmed older, white, union-hall Democrats who no longer felt at home in their own party. Securing not much more than a third of the popular vote and just seventeen electoral college votes, McGovern's antiwar campaign plunged to defeat in November.

The Watergate Scandal

Many Democrats loathed Richard Nixon for his early Red-baiting career, and quite a few certainly danced with delight as the disgraced "Tricky Dick" gave one last grandiose salute from the steps of his helicopter in August 1974 (above). His resignation concluded multiple investigations into whether he ordered the June 1972 break-in at the Democratic National Committee offices in the Watergate Hotel. Chaired by Senator Sam Ervin, televised Senate hearings in the summer of 1973 built up a picture of an administration with absolutely no scruples over committing corrupt and criminal acts to further its partisan interests. In the spring of 1972, for instance, paid "dirty tricksters" had forged Democratic press releases, set off stink bombs at Democratic gatherings, and falsely accused potentially competitive Democratic presidential contenders like Senator Henry Jackson of sexual impropriety. When asked to supply what he knew were damaging taped conversations, Nixon pleaded executive privilege—a rule that allows the president to deny access to sensitive White House documents in the national interest—and he forced the sacking of special prosecutor Archibald Cox on October 20,1973. After trying to release edited versions, Nixon grudgingly handed over the full tapes on August 5. Four days later he finally resigned to avoid impeachment, leaving all politicians, not just Republicans, tainted by his actions.

Breach of Trust

The Washington Post (owned by Katharine Graham, above right) played a central role in the unfolding story of Watergate and set a new standard for investigative journalism. The repeated revelation of politicians' lies not only created a public demand for Nixon's impeachment (top), but led people to become deeply cynical about their motives. They would not trust later presidents the way they had FDR, Harry Truman, or Jack Kennedy. When new president Gerald Ford (above left) granted a pardon to Nixon, few believed Ford's protestations that this was a genuine attempt to heal the nation by bringing closure to the Watergate scandal. It smacked of being just another deal.

"My name is Jimmy Carter...

...and I'm running for president."
Before the 1976 primaries, few outside
of Georgia had heard of Jimmy Carter.
In the aftermath of Watergate,
however, this was a large part of his
appeal. He was the polar opposite of
the now-suspect Washington insider
and reawakened the party's populist
core vote (above right). Carter also
embodied the New South as a white
politician able to appeal to the region's
new interracial electorate. With Walter
Mondale (above left) to strengthen his
ties to the traditional national party—
especially organized labor—Carter
defeated Gerald Ford by a slim margin,
just 297 to 240 in the electoral college.
On a bright but cold Inauguration
Day, the new president with his wife,
Rosalyn, tried to show that they
remained on the same level as the
people. Instead of sweeping past in a
limousine, they walked and waved to
the crowds (right).

Peace, War, and Religion

Even critics applauded when President Carter brokered the Camp David peace agreement. Formally, the 1973 Middle East War had never ended, and Israel continued to occupy Egypt's Sinai peninsula. At the president's Maryland retreat, Carter—a devout Christian—used his sensitivity to religious feeling to induce Egyptian president Anwar Sadat (left) to recognize Israeli sovereignty and Israeli premier Menachem Begin (right) to return Sinai to Egypt. A three-way handshake sealed the deal. But Carter completely misread the mood of Islamic public opinion in Iran. There, the prominent Shiite cleric Ayatollah Khomeini (above) had turned anger against the shah into a successful revolution in January 1979. When Carter allowed the exiled shah to receive cancer treatment in the U.S., a mob stormed the U.S Embassy in Tehran and took fifty-three hostages on November 4, 1979. Khomeini's demand that the U.S. return the shah and all Iranian assets in return for the hostages' release dominated Carter's final year in office.

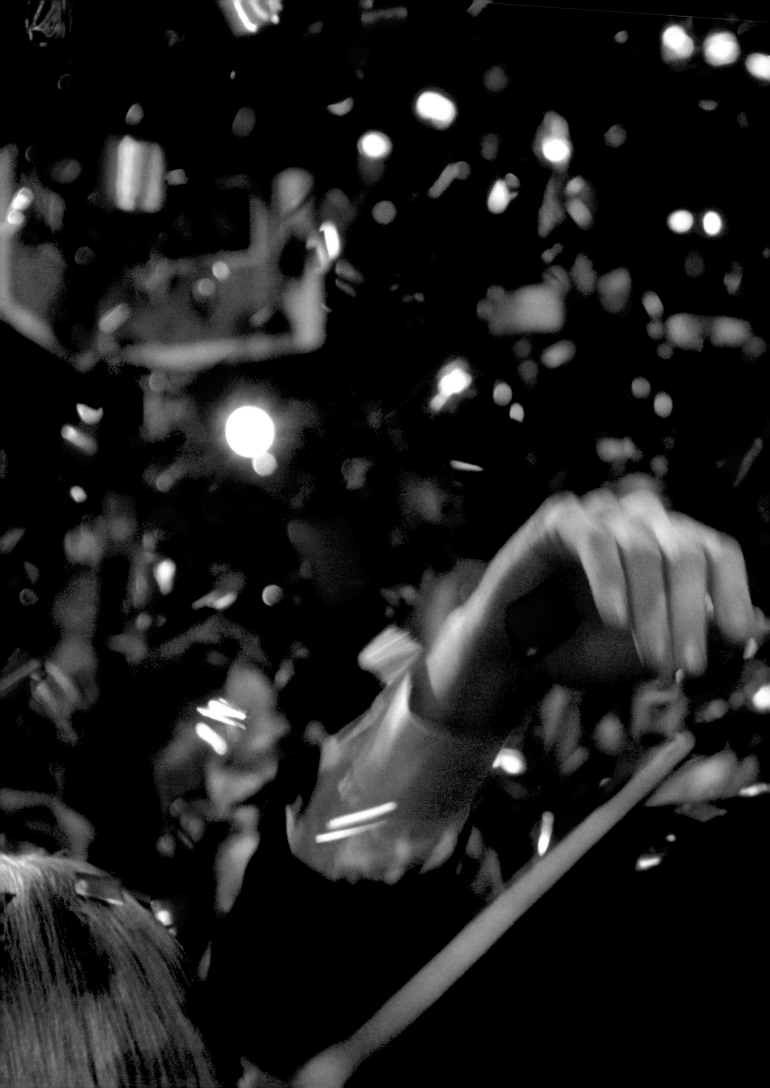

Chapter Seven

A New Kind of Democrat

1981–2003

A New Kind of Democrat
1981–2003

JIMMY CARTER NEVER BONDED with the Democratic Party leadership. Against the backdrop of Watergate, he had run against the Washington establishment and by 1980 he had antagonized both liberals and conservatives. The Left denounced his increased defense spending and support for the shah of Iran, and the Right complained about his anticorporate appointments to regulatory agencies and weakness toward the Soviets. Labor was appalled when he refused to back the Humphrey-Hawkins Full Employment Bill, which would have made full employment a mandated priority for the federal government, and environmentalists shuddered when he deregulated the oil industry. The most conservative Democratic president since Grover Cleveland, Carter had a similar effect on the Democrats' electoral fortunes. In November he carried just six states, and the party lost twelve Senate and thirty-three House seats. The electorate wanted less federal government, a more assertive foreign policy, and a clearer commitment to traditional moral values; in short, if not a Republican, then a new kind of Democrat.

It was a painful message that the party was slow to understand. Carter's vice president, Walter Mondale, an old-style liberal with close ties to organized labor, won the 1984 nomination. To the traditional campaign cry that the Republicans were rewarding the rich and ignoring the poor, he added an appeal to women. But despite selecting Geraldine Ferraro as his running mate, the first woman on a major party presidential ticket, he carried just one state. One of the few highlights of a disastrous campaign was Mario Cuomo's convention speech. He spoke eloquently of the needs of ordinary people that were ignored in Reagan's America and described how he had risen from a poor immigrant family to become governor of New York. Cuomo seemed to embody a political trend to which Democrats must respond. Immigrants from southern and eastern Europe, who had first rallied politically around FDR in the 1930s, were now solid, middle-class citizens. Just as JFK's election had been a watershed for Irish Americans in 1960, so another ethnic nominee could renew support for the Democrats among these established immigrants.

A depressed economy and international setbacks ensured few Americans smiled with President Carter in 1980.

Previous page: Kennedy but with a Dixie twist: Bill Clinton became the first Democratic president since FDR to win reelection in 1996, but only by being a new kind of Democrat.

Challengers Gary Hart and Jesse Jackson may have hurt Walter Mondale in 1984 by squeezing his appeal to morally conservative white voters.

The defeated 1984 Democratic ticket was the first to feature a woman, as Geraldine Ferraro took the vice presidential slot.

In 1988 Governor Michael Dukakis of Massachusetts, a Greek American, won the nomination. His selection and subsequent defeat revealed deep problems for the Democrats. The nomination race had become a prolonged ordeal in the media spotlight that was costly both financially and politically. The primaries began in New Hampshire—a profoundly unrepresentative state—and by the time they reached the South, numerous candidates had been weakened. They had insufficient money left to spread their message and/or they had publicly committed themselves to policy positions unpopular in the key Sunbelt states— California, Texas, and Florida. In Colorado Senator Gary Hart's case, the media exposed private embarrassments, as he had rashly challenged them to do: most famously, the married senator's encounter with a model aboard the appropriately named yacht, *Monkey Business*.

The 1988 campaign was Jesse Jackson's career peak. A former associate of Martin Luther King, Jackson surprised commentators by his primary successes as he urged Democrats to join his Rainbow Coalition. He appealed most to his fellow African Americans, but his aim was also to boost participation among the new wave of Hispanic and Asian immigrants who had entered the U.S. after the 1965 Immigration Act. Needing every vote, Dukakis felt he had to fund Jackson's plans to get out the votes of the Rainbow Coalition across the nation in November. He also allowed Jackson a prominent role at the convention.

Dukakis tried to placate moderates by putting respected conservative Lloyd Bentsen of Texas on the ticket and by steadfastly refusing to call himself a liberal, or even use the "L" word. But Jackson's conspicuous presence amplified Republican claims. Using negative advertising about his stance on school prayer and lenient treatment of prisoners, the GOP sold the idea that beneath Dukakis's buttoned-down, "geek" persona, lurked a McGovern-style radical. By October only 22 percent of Americans regarded George H. W. Bush as too conservative compared to 37 percent who felt that Dukakis was too liberal to make a good president. On election day Bush carried forty states. Gloomily, Senator Sam Nunn of the centrist Democratic Leadership Council (DLC) warned: "If our appeal is to the dispossessed, we'll get only the dispossessed to vote for us… Every time you attempt to go left, you will bring out at least equal numbers of voters against you on the right."

As the inauguration of yet another Republican president neared in January 1989, veteran Democrat Joseph Califano offered hard advice to his colleagues. Democrats had better think hard about why "so many whites perceive us as the party of blacks and special interests, soft on crime and naive about defense." As long as that perception lasted, Califano insisted, then the party would inevitably languish. Almost immediately after the election, columnist Jefferson Morley had said much the same thing. Democrats, he wrote, "must turn to national leaders who can perform comfortably in the culture of poor and middle-income Southern whites, like…Bill Clinton of Arkansas."

This was a remarkable prediction, since Clinton had made a turgid summer convention speech that was still stale in Democratic memories. But William Jefferson Clinton deserved his nickname, "the Comeback Kid." Elected governor of Arkansas in 1978, he had lost his 1980 reelection bid because he had increased motor vehicle taxes. It was a mistake he never repeated. For the next two years he repeatedly apologized and made alliances with powerful local business interests, while his wife, Hillary Rodham Clinton, concentrated on building up a lucrative legal practice with real estate interests. As a child Bill had attended black church services and socialized with African Americans, an unusual thing for a Southern white boy in the 1960s. Among white politicians he seemed to have an unrivaled rapport with black voters. Reelected in 1982, he joined a moderate group that included Arkansas senator Dale Bumpers, Georgia senator Sam Nunn, and Tennessee senator Al Gore, who founded the Democratic Leadership Council. With political consultant Dick Morris's help, he remained governor for another ten years and acquired a national profile heading the DLC.

When the 1992 race began, Clinton came in second to Massachusetts senator Paul Tsongas in New Hampshire. But he hung on and gathered momentum through his victories in simultaneous Southern primaries on "Super Tuesday." Key victories in Illinois and New York locked up the nomination well before the convention. Meanwhile, Clinton had already set about dispelling the Dukakis legacy. To show just how tough he was on crime, he flew back to Little Rock during the New Hampshire primary to underline his backing for the execution of Ricky Ray Rector, a convicted killer with an IQ of just 64. To distance himself from Jesse Jackson, he denounced rap singer Sister Souljah, whom Jackson had invited to his Chicago rally. After the 1991 Los Angeles riots in response to the videotaped beating of Rodney King, she had commented that, given the black-on-black killings endemic to gang life, things might improve if the gangs only killed whites for a week. Clinton publicly told Jackson that he should not provide a platform for someone "filled with a kind of hatred that you do not honor."

Slain heroes Lincoln, JFK, Bobby Kennedy, and Martin Luther King adorn this 1988 Democratic Convention button. It failed to inspire victory.

Mike and Kitty Dukakis's bid for the White House failed because of voter apathy (half did not bother to vote) and a negative Republican ad campaign.

Events favored Clinton. The 1991 Gulf War victory surprisingly failed to help President Bush, because the immediate euphoria had been dissipated by economic bad news. Unemployment stood at 7.6 percent by summer 1992. Median household income was still sliding from 1989 levels, while medical costs had rocketed. The federal deficit had jumped to a staggering $290 billion, and Bush, despite his celebrated "Read my lips: No new taxes" pledge, had raised taxes to the fury of Republican hard-liners. Trying to appease them, he allowed conservatives to dominate the Republican convention. Their extremist rhetoric, particularly over abortion, alarmed liberals who might otherwise have abstained. He was also helped by the maverick third-party candidacy of millionaire Ross Perot over the deficit issue. Clinton carried thirty states to defeat Bush by 353 to 132 electoral college votes.

Clinton began his presidency badly with a succession of botched appointments and a furor over his proposed relaxation of policy on gays in the military. He had boasted that his cabinet would "look like America," which in practice meant more women and minorities. Two female nominees were rejected before Clinton could appoint the first female attorney general, Janet Reno. A leading black female lawyer, Lani Guinier, was nominated to head the Civil Rights Division of the Justice Department, despite the fact that she had written controversial articles proposing constitutional safeguards for African American group rights. Congressional misgivings forced Clinton to withdraw her nomination. Opposition from Sam Nunn, head of the Senate Armed Services Committee, and General Colin Powell, chair of the Joint Chiefs, to Clinton's executive order ending discrimination against homosexuality in the armed forces pushed him to adopt a dubious compromise policy of "don't ask, don't tell." It left both sides of the debate aggrieved.

Within five days of taking office, Clinton appointed his wife Hillary to head the health-care reform task force. Senior Democrats on Capitol Hill, like Senator Daniel Moynihan, argued that health reform should logically follow welfare reform, which, during the election, Clinton had also recognized as essential. When the task force reported in September, it offered universal health insurance through competing private health plans. Most Americans would be covered via new health maintenance organizations (HMOs). Predictably, the plan faced criticism from all sides. Small businesses—increasingly seen as vital to job creation—rebelled at the idea of paying 80 percent of employees' premiums. Medium and small insurance companies feared being squeezed out of

Hillary Clinton's appointment to head the health-care reform task force expanded the role of First Lady but proved a risky investment of the president's political capital.

the health sector entirely, and the medical lobby fed fears that patients would no longer be able to choose their doctor. Clinton needed to compromise, but he refused Senate Minority Leader Bob Dole's offer to work for one and doomed the project. Only sustained economic recovery ensured that the electorate ignored this failure.

Even more risky for Clinton's reelection was his endorsement of NAFTA, Bush's 1992 North American Free Trade Agreement. It had no safeguards against U.S. companies relocating jobs to low-wage Mexico, where their plants would not need to meet costly environmental standards. Just the threat of relocation could win concessions from already weakened American unions. Clinton's swift approval of a new General Agreement on Tariffs and Trade (GATT) confirmed his free trade fixation. "Open and competitive commerce," he enthused, "will enrich us as a nation… In the face of all the pressures to do the reverse, we must compete, not retreat."

Heading into the midterm elections, Clinton had alienated organized labor, environmentalists, and liberals in Congress. He had not delivered a middle-class tax cut nor pushed either health care or welfare reform through Congress. The highbrow media was investigating a dubious property deal back in Arkansas, which became known as the "Whitewater scandal," while the tabloids eagerly took up the cause of Paula Jones. She sued the president for damages when he denied sexually propositioning her in a Little Rock hotel room in 1991. Foolishly, Clinton failed to offer Jones a large enough financial proposition to keep her mouth shut. When he spoke of powerful forces threatening to bring down his administration, talk-show host Jay Leno quipped, "I think they're called hormones." It did not take long memories for voters to associate this latest Clinton sexual imbroglio with the Gennifer Flowers claims that had surfaced when he was running for president, and which Clinton had successfully skirted in an interview.

With conservatives in full cry in 1994 and over 60 percent of voters declining to participate in the elections, control of Congress passed to the Republicans for the first time since 1952. Democratic casualties included House Speaker Thomas Foley and Governors Mario Cuomo of New York and Ann Richards of Texas. Those Democrats who survived tended to be liberals with little reason to like or trust their president. There seemed no way back for Clinton.

On April 19, 1995, Timothy McVeigh, an ex-serviceman with right-wing militia ties, planted a bomb in a federal office building in Oklahoma City. It claimed 168 lives, including children in a basement nursery. Clinton eloquently articulated the nation's pain and anger at the funeral,

Madeleine Albright, America's first woman and first Jewish secretary of state, was one of Clinton's later and most effective female appointments.

If only it had stopped at hugs! President Clinton's affair with Monica Lewinsky would tarnish his entire presidency.

Special Prosecutor Kenneth Starr's pursuit of the president was so blatantly partisan that it offended many Americans' sense of privacy and decency.

and linked the incident to the hard-line rhetoric of right-wing Republican groups. Guided by pollster Dick Morris, he seized the Republican issue of deficit reduction by submitting a budget that would gradually balance and provide tax cuts for middle-income groups. He also mended his relationship with organized labor, whose new leader, John Sweeney, recognized the Republican threat. The AFL-CIO asked its members for $25 million to support candidates opposed to Newt Gingrich's "Contract with America." During budget negotiations, Republican crassness on Capitol Hill forced parts of the federal government to shut down temporarily due to lack of funds. Voters began to regard the GOP as extremist, and Clinton's ratings climbed rapidly.

Clinton also began to score some foreign policy successes. He supported the Oslo Accords between Israel and the Palestine Liberation Organization. Aware of popular misgivings about any commitment of U.S. ground forces since Vietnam, he intervened tentatively in Bosnia but then committed 20,000 troops as peacekeepers to ensure Slobodan Milosevic of Serbia abided by the Dayton Agreement. His remarkable 1996 comeback, however, just like his 1992 victory, stemmed mainly from the economy. The stock market boomed, corporate profits soared, unemployment fell, inflation was minimal, and interest rates were stable. Needing to appear reasonable, Republicans approved Clinton's increase in the minimum wage. Playing to public prejudices about the unworthy poor, he had promised in 1992 "to end welfare as we know it." In late July 1996, despite publicly recognizing its serious flaws, he signed a welfare reform law that ended the federal commitment to aid families with dependent children. This was a New Deal measure that Franklin Roosevelt had secured in 1936. Primary responsibility for the delivery of time-limited welfare payments returned to the individual states.

In November, less than half of the eligible electorate bothered to vote, but they gave Clinton a comfortable 379 to 159 victory in the electoral college over the uninspiring Bob Dole. There were mutterings about the president's character during the election when questions arose over his fundraising techniques. Donors had bought time in the Lincoln bedroom, for instance, and Far Eastern contributors in particular seemed to have bought influence on trade policy.

The booming economy brought a balanced budget within reach during Clinton's second term, allowing Democrats to counter Republican demands for tax cuts with calls for investment in education, welfare, health, and national infrastructure. But barely a year after his second inaugural, Clinton faced a fresh scandal on the familiar theme of his sexual misconduct. Claims surfaced that he had been having a furtive sexual relationship with a young White House intern, Monica Lewinsky. Clinton denied having had "sexual relations with that woman," a phrase that, it later emerged, had a narrow legal definition for the president. More calamitously, Clinton repeated his denial in a deposition for the ongoing Paula Jones case, and a written affidavit from Lewinsky backed his story. Special Prosecutor Kenneth Starr, appointed initially to investigate Whitewater, had taped conversations from a Lewinsky confidante, Linda Tripp, that suggested both president and aide were lying under oath. He asked and received permission to widen his investigation. As the titillating saga unfolded, the grotesque prospect of impeachment grew.

Both the incessant polls and the 1998 midterm election returns suggested that the American people did not believe that Clinton's overactive libido and inactive moral compass disqualified him from office. Barely 36 percent of the electorate bothered to vote in 1998—the lowest turnout since the war election of 1942. Reelected as governor of Texas, George W. Bush became the favorite for the Republican nomination in 2000. Democrats consoled themselves that their five gains in the House were seeds of recovery. The country was weary of the Lewinsky affair, but the partisanship ensured that articles of impeachment passed the House in December for trial before the Senate in January 1999. After thirty-seven days of legal wrangling, no charges secured a majority.

Clinton apologized to the nation for his lapse but did not seem truly repentant. His last budget committed the huge projected surpluses largely to deficit reduction, but proposed a significant increase in defense spending and in funding for Medicare and other entitlement programs. Bidding for the Democratic nomination, liberal Bill Bradley charged that programs for people should take precedence over debt repayment. Clinton's heir, Al Gore, responded that even during a recession he would honor debt reduction commitments. By ensuring Gore the nomination on Super Tuesday, March 7, 2000, Democrats seemed to endorse this return to Grover Cleveland–style fiscal discipline.

As the campaign intensified, Gore sensed that he needed to consolidate his environmentalist support because polls showed that Ralph Nader was likely to attract 7 percent of voters to his Green Party. Most of these would be disgruntled Democrats, and their loss might spell defeat in a close contest. More intractable was the plain fact that Gore came across as dull. When he kissed his wife fervently at the

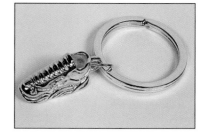

Defeated Democratic contender Bill Bradley graciously gave Tiffany key rings as a thank-you to the media corps and members of his 2000 campaign staff.

"Chads"—the word on everybody's lips in November 2000, as the post-election wrangling descended into near farce.

Joseph Lieberman could become America's first Jewish president in 2004, and this campaign yarmulke is in the best traditions of Democratic campaign headgear.

convention, it appeared so out of character that it made the news. Meanwhile, Bush, despite public lapses in his knowledge of international relations and a seeming difficulty in wrestling with the English language, gathered support. He aped Clinton's centrist rhetoric at an orchestrated Republican Convention that promised "to put conservative values and conservative ideas into the thick of the fight for justice and opportunity." By November half the electorate was too bored to vote, and the other half gave Gore a 539,000-vote lead in the popular vote. But by carrying Florida by a margin of less than a thousand votes, Bush seemed to have won an electoral college majority. However, numerous irregularities emerged due to variations in ballot design, the failure of Florida ballot machines to punch through cleanly, and official discrimination in largely black, and therefore predominantly Democratic, precincts. On December 4, 2000, however, the U.S. Supreme Court overruled a court ruling that had allowed Gore to insist on a hand recount in several counties. With the clock stopped with Bush still leading by 537 votes in Florida, Gore conceded.

Paul Taylor, Reuters diplomatic editor, assessed Bush's first 100 days thus: "In just 14 weeks, he has angered China, cold-shouldered Russia, humiliated South Korea, worried Japan, dismayed the Arab world, irritated the European Union, outraged environmentalists and snubbed campaigners for global justice." At home the stock market fell and a flagging economy made the personal and corporate debt from the 1990s alarming. Democrats felt that Bush was destined to be a one-term president like his father, but their calculations had to be redrawn after the September 11 attacks. A shocked nation rallied around its president, and Americans demanded that their leaders unite and fight back against the terrorist threat. Democrats backed the war in Afghanistan, and with more misgiving, they supported the war against Iraq.

The 2002 elections had returned Congress to Republican control, and the Democratic contenders for 2004 seemed uninspiring. Senator John Kerry of Nebraska and Governor Howard Dean of Vermont were worthy. Longtime House Leader Dick Gephardt had name recognition, and black protest leader Al Sharpton had eclipsed Jesse Jackson. For those relying on the Southern factor, there was Senator John Edwards of North Carolina, while others felt that the 2000 vice presidential choice, Joseph Lieberman, could rally the party. It said all too much about the state of the party that many regretted Al Gore's refusal to run, and no one doubted that we would one day hear again from the junior senator from New York, Hillary Rodham Clinton.

Made for TV, 1981

With dignity and a more convincing smile than his wife Rosalyn could manage, President Carter posed on election day with incoming President Ronald Reagan and new First Lady, Nancy. Reagan's sure sense of where the camera was and Nancy's fur trim were just two clues that the Republican victors would bring a different approach to the presidency. Carter had applied his formidable intelligence to the problems of government, but his rational approach had not enabled him to end stagflation or deal with Iranian militants. As he boarded Air Force One as a defeated president (top left), a plane landed with the hostages from the U.S. Embassy in Tehran (bottom left). Carter had tried everything to secure their release, including a failed military rescue mission, and had agreed terms with Iran weeks earlier. Their homecoming was his achievement, but was made to seem Reagan's victory.

1984: The Old Party and the New Woman

Like his mentor, Hubert Humphrey, Minnesota's Walter
Mondale (above) was a product of the old Democratic
Party, of FDR's New Deal coalition of organized labor,
white urban ethnics, Northern blacks, and—uneasily—
the white South. By 1984, however, the party had lost
white urban support, the South had changed, and
union ranks had dwindled. The party seemed to have
lost its moorings. It hoped that by having a woman on
the ticket it might boost support among female voters
(right). In November, however, Geraldine Ferraro
(opposite, with Mondale) could not protect Mondale
from the Reagan deluge. He held on to just thirteen
electoral college votes.

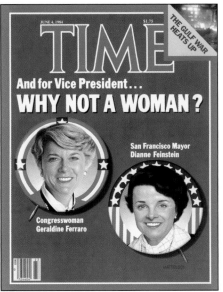

Either Too Hot or Too Cold

In the early phases of the 1988 primary campaign, Colorado senator Gary Hart had emerged as a front-runner. Handsome and articulate, he seemed to herald a return to the heady days of Kennedy mania. Unfortunately for him, the sexual antics that the press turned a blind eye to in the 1950s, it photographed and syndicated in the 1980s. Exposed as an adulterer, an apologetic Hart withdrew from the race (left). This left the way open for Governor Michael Dukakis of Massachusetts, a product of the same state as Jack Kennedy, but with none of his style. He came over as cold rather than cool. Even adding Texan Lloyd Bentsen to the ticket (below) could not ensure a reprise of 1960.

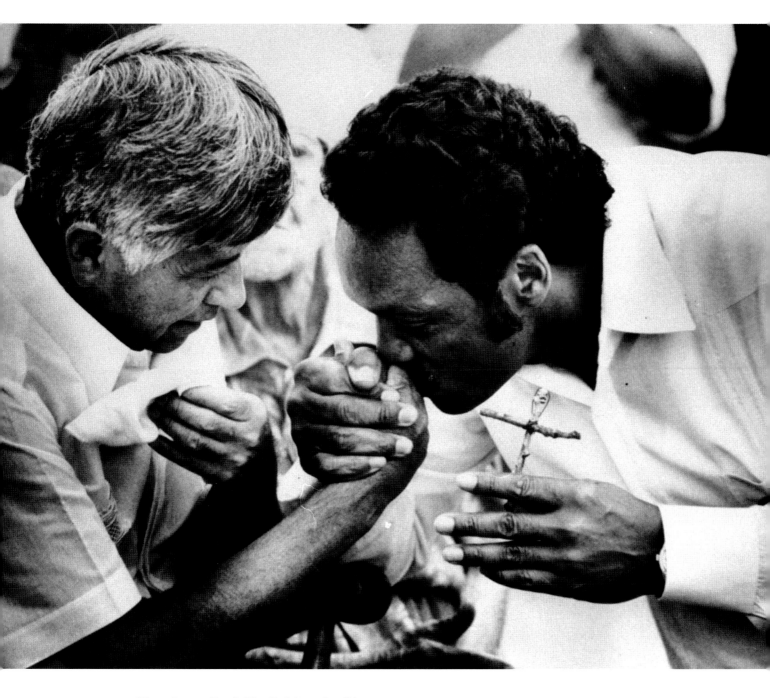

"Run, Jesse, Run": The Rainbow Coalition

By 1988 the African American vote had become for the Democratic Party what the AFL-CIO had once been: a core constituency. Black voters tended to vote Democrat, but their influence depended heavily on a high turnout. The appeal of Jesse Jackson's primary campaign for party officials consisted chiefly of the boost it would give to voter registration and turnout among African Americans. To them, Jackson was a maverick, having never previously been elected to political office on the Democratic ticket. Jackson (with legendary Chicano labor leader Cesar Chavez, above) couched his campaign in terms of mobilizing not just blacks but other minorities, especially Hispanics, to create a "Rainbow Coalition" of the poor. From such a foundation, the Democrats could mount an orthodox attack on Republican greed.

1988: Three Strikes Against

Michael Dukakis (left) wanted to be seen as a businesslike Democrat— a technically astute, well-informed executive who could manage the economy and foreign policy through expertise. "Trust me," he seemed to say, "I look like a doctor." With inflation and unemployment relatively low, Americans were unsure if they needed Dukakis's medicine. While the Dukakis camp tried to avoid controversy, George Bush's team rallied their Republican core vote by playing up Dukakis's liberalism on what pollsters call "hot button" items like the death penalty and patriotism. A sad omen of a third consecutive Democratic defeat was the fact that the debate between

vice-presidential candidates Democrat Lloyd Bentsen and Republican Dan Quayle (above, left and right respectively) was a bigger news story than the tedious debates between Dukakis and Bush. With a gift for media gaffes, the youthful Quayle boasted that he had as much congressional experience as JFK did when he contested the presidency in 1960. Bentsen's response to the implied comparison was memorably crushing. "I knew Jack Kennedy," he said, adding with a dismissive shake of the head, "Senator, you're no Jack Kennedy." But even the idea of Quayle being a heartbeat away from the presidency did not stop voters from choosing Bush over Dukakis in November.

Why Didn't They Do Something?

By the end of the 1980s the policies of the Republicans—cutting taxes and reducing welfare—had created a nation in which the richer were getting ostentatiously richer and the poorest were equally conspicuously sinking into a level of destitution not seen since the 1930s (opposite, a grimly familiar sight in New York and other cities). The spectacle of widespread homelessness in major metropolitan areas should have created the ideal political climate for Democratic leadership. For various reasons, leading Democrats did not seize their chance. Senator Edward Kennedy of Massachusetts (top left), while still enjoying some support due to his family name and distinguished Senate career, had vainly challenged incumbent Jimmy Carter for the nomination in 1980, but seemed to retire into the role of senior senator thereafter. Only family scandal or tragedy seemed to bring him out. Equally distinguished, Senator Patrick Moynihan of New York (center left) was highly regarded as a policy analyst but mistrusted across the party as a maverick because of his work in the Nixon administration. The Democrat who best articulated anger at Republican rule was probably Governor Mario Cuomo of New York. In his 1984 address to the Democratic National Convention, Cuomo lambasted the grotesque inequalities of people's lives in Reagan's America and articulated a vision of government as the guarantor of individual dignity and decency. Building on that speech, Cuomo could have rallied a second New Deal coalition. Yet he never took up FDR's mantle; he never tried to follow his illustrious predecessor's hugely significant journey from the governor's mansion in Albany to the White House.

The Racial Fault Line

On March 3, 1991, four white Los Angeles police officers were caught on video inflicting a savage beating on an African American motorist, Rodney King (top left). Despite this evidence, widely shown on national television, just over a year later an all-white suburban Los Angeles jury cleared the police of all charges. In outrage at what seemed a flagrant injustice, the predominantly black South Central section of Los Angeles exploded in an orgy of destruction that left many buildings razed to the ground (above). Most frightening of all for many Americans, a traffic surveillance camera filmed a white truck driver being pulled from his cab and beaten mercilessly by African American assailants (bottom left). The racial and ethnic tensions that fed into these disturbances were complex, setting black and certain Hispanic groups against not just whites but new Asian immigrants as well.

Choosing Bill Clinton

By 1992 the run of presidential defeats had prompted concerned party leaders to establish the Democratic Leadership Council to develop a winning strategy. Southerners, including Governor Bill Clinton of Arkansas, dominated the DLC. Clinton's first objective was to put in a respectable performance in New Hampshire against favorite Paul Tsongas (above). He achieved this and also got around questions about dodging the Vietnam draft and smoking marijuana. Clinton went on to win the Southern primaries on "Super Tuesday," which ensured him the nomination. He chose Tennessee's Al Gore, who had a military record and a clean image, as running mate. Gore's wife, Tipper (with Hillary Rodham Clinton, right), had campaigned against obscenity in pop music lyrics. Thus her national profile paralleled the campaign prominence of Hillary. With the economy souring, Clinton was rightly confident that he could give George Bush the boot in November (opposite).

Happy Days Are Here Again?

Presentation was supposedly the Clinton team's forte. But one columnist sniped that the 1993 inaugural events made him wonder whether he was watching a Las Vegas act or a hundred Super Bowl halftime shows. There was no hint of Jimmy Carter's walk with the people as the line of stretch limousines reached Reaganite proportions. The happy First Couple (left) greeted old associates and celebrities with 1,000-watt smiles. The first baby-boomer president, Clinton had soul diva Aretha Franklin (above) perform from the steps of the Lincoln Memorial, as did Marian Anderson so memorably more than half a century before.

Pleasing No One

The early years of the Clinton administration disappointed. His early executive order relaxing the ban on homosexual relations in the armed forces drew fire from the head of the Joint Chiefs of Staff, Colin Powell, and Chair of the Senate Armed Service Committee, Sam Nunn (above right). His revised position that authorities should not ask about and service personnel should not tell of their homosexual relations outraged the gay community (below right). Despite demands from powerful Democrats like Congressman Richard Gephardt (above), who feared U.S. job losses, Clinton chose to sign the North American Free Trade Agreement negotiated by the Bush administration. Most damaging, under Hillary Clinton's leadership (left) the administration failed to deliver health care reform in 1994. In the midterm elections of that year, Republicans captured both houses for the first time since 1952. Clinton looked doomed.

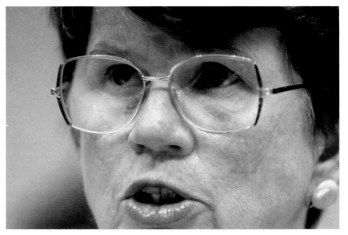

Feeling the People's Pain

In the spring of 1995 a deeply alienated former soldier, Timothy McVeigh, planted a bomb that destroyed the federal office building in Oklahoma City (above left), killing nearly 200. He claimed to be taking revenge for an FBI attack on the Branch Davidian compound at Waco, Texas, exactly two years earlier (far left), which had been ordered by Attorney General Janet Reno (left). McVeigh's action shocked Americans who wondered what could cause a previously loyal American to turn upon his fellow citizens in this way. As president, Bill Clinton rose to the occasion and eloquently expressed the nation's sorrow and his own (above, with Hillary planting a dogwood tree in the White House lawn to honor the victims). More significantly, Clinton placed McVeigh's actions in the context of the rhetoric of right-wing political extremists who had, on the radio and over the Internet, promulgated conspiracy theories and fomented hatred.

The Comeback of 1996

For most of his first term, Bill Clinton had struggled to pass his policies in the face of a hostile Republican Congress. The climax came in a series of budgetary clashes. The loquacious Republican Speaker Newt Gingrich (top left) had drafted his "Contract with America" for the 1994 elections. This was a hard-line conservative manifesto that made more centrist figures like Bob Dole (behind Gingrich) uneasy. Pressing for deeper cuts in federal spending, Gingrich failed to ensure continuing appropriations when no budget was

agreed for 1995–96. As a result, much of the federal government had to shut down on two separate occasions. This made Americans more appreciative of what the federal government did and enabled environmental activists (bottom left), among others, to warn that cutting back on government might have devastating consequences. As a result, by the time Bill Clinton (above) faced Dole in November 1996, he was well ahead in the polls and striding confidently to victory.

A Sea of Scandal

When Bill Clinton emerged as the Democratic nominee in 1992, Republican strategists suggested that he might be vulnerable on the character issue. Initially, questions rose about his evasion of military service, and he earned laughter rather than trust by claiming that when it came to marijuana use, he may have smoked but he had never inhaled. More serious problems, however, erupted toward the end of his first year in office, when an ongoing investigation into the collapse of Arkansas savings and loans companies drew attention to Hillary Clinton's role in a dubious development scheme called "Whitewater." Subpoenaed to testify, the First Lady (right) was sufficiently embroiled to justify the appointment of a special prosecutor. Around the same time, rumors about President Clinton's past sexual escapades crystallized in the form of Gennifer Flowers (harking back to 1992 allegations) and Paula Jones. Both complained loudly about Clinton's ungentlemanly conduct and about conspiracies to suppress the truth. Eventually, Jones would receive an all-too-belated—though pleasing—financial settlement (above left, her moment of vindication), while Flowers (below left) was able to punctuate her nightclub singing with book-signings and talk show appearances.

Republicans' Revenge

Unable to find grounds for prosecution over Whitewater, Special Prosecutor Kenneth Starr (left) proved ready, even eager, to follow the salacious trail that led from the Oval Office to White House intern Monica Lewinsky (below left). Clinton denied having sexual relations with young Monica: once to the American people on television, and once under oath, during depositions taken in connection with the Paula Jones case. As this was a lie, Starr could therefore prove that the president was guilty of perjury. Accordingly, but to the dismay of many Americans, Republicans in Congress pressed for impeachment. The Democratic leadership recognized that Clinton had shown poor judgment and demeaned his office, and they were prepared to support a strong censure motion. The vindictive impeachment proceedings ended with no charges being carried and with a suitably hangdog expression, the president (opposite) apologized to the nation and his family.

Foreign Ties and Diplomatic Tangles

The fall of the Soviet Union in 1989 required successive presidents to develop a formula for international stability that was not framed by the polarities of the cold war. George Bush had adopted a largely "wait-and-see" stance toward the new Russia, but Bill Clinton took a chance and actively backed Boris Yeltsin (opposite). He obviously believed that he could see eye to eye with this mercurial bear of a man. As the one remaining superpower, the United States was expected to lead the way diplomatically, especially in volatile areas like the Middle East. Getting (above, from left to right)

Yitzhak Rabin of Israel, Habny Mubarak of Egypt, King Hussein of Jordan, and Yasser Arafat of the Palestine Liberation Organization into the same room had the potential to straighten out more than ties. The agreement signed at this 1995 meeting gave the Palestinians limited self-rule in the Gaza Strip and West Bank city of Jericho. Tragically, just as the Camp David Accords prompted Egyptian hard-liners to murder Anwar Sadat, so these concessions spurred a Jewish zealot to assassinate Rabin in late 1995.

The Gore Campaign

Although Bill Clinton was expected to leave a buoyant economy with the federal deficit transformed into a projected surplus, he did not really provide his vice president, Al Gore, with a winning inheritance. The Lewinsky scandal ensured that Gore tried to keep Clinton at arm's length as the 2000 campaign began. Equally significantly, the Clinton administration had adopted Republican positions and compromised on the defense of social welfare programs. This made traditional Democrats mistrustful of the idea that Social Security and Medicare would be safe under a Democratic president (top left). The general view was that Gore was worthy but dull, and as a team, he and Joseph Lieberman (center left) were hardly likely to set the party faithful's pulses racing. In 1992 Gore had made environmentalism a part of his appeal, but in 2000 he faced a serious challenge from Green Party candidate Ralph Nader (bottom left), who might drain crucial support in a close race. Gore's main asset seemed most likely to be his opponent, Texan George W. Bush, who to Democratic loyalists (right) combined Ronald Reagan's intellectual depth and close knowledge of world affairs with Richard Nixon's charm.

Overleaf: Gore and Clinton have something to smile about, having just announced publicly that the administration's budget has been passed by Congress on October 15, 1998.

A Bad Day for Democracy

Historians are bound to scrutinize the 2000 election, but as an example of democracy at work it hardly bears contemplating. In a close race, more Americans voted for Al Gore than for George Bush but the president, of course, is elected not directly by the people, but by the electoral college, and Gore did not have a clear majority there. History was on hold, the newspapers declared (above), as the contest hinged in 2000—as it had in 1876—on the outcome in Florida, whose governor, Jeb Bush, just happened to be the brother of the Republican presidential candidate. On November 27 Gore announced that he would contest the Florida result (left). The unfolding story of the Florida count raised questions about the validity of any result. Worn-out, defective ballot machines had left a crucial number of ballots unclearly marked, even under close scrutiny (right). Two issues gradually emerged from weeks of legal challenge and counterchallenge. First, could hand counting ensure a consistent standard of interpretation, and second, if applied in one county, should it not be applied in all? With little prospect of an election result, these grounds were used by a Republican-dominated U.S. Supreme Court to stop the count in Florida and effectively hand the presidency to George Walker Bush.

The 2004 Race: Early Runners

The September 11 attacks and the subsequent wars in Afghanistan and Iraq have changed the tenor of national politics and given the Republican incumbent, President Bush, a potentially strong position. Some Democrats, like Al Gore, have ruled themselves out, and others, like Hillary Clinton (bottom left), seem content to wait for a later race. Nevertheless, the contest for the nomination already features familiar figures. House Majority Leader Richard Gephardt (opposite, top left), 2000 vice-presidential nominee Joseph Lieberman (opposite, bottom right), and Senator John Kerry of Massachusetts (top left) are in the frame. Governor Howard Dean of Vermont (opposite, top right) as the traditional New Englander will expect to do well in New Hampshire, while Southerner Senator John Edwards of North Carolina (opposite, bottom left), will pin his hopes on the primaries of Super Tuesday. African American maverick Al Sharpton (center left) will see if his New York notoriety can grow on the national stage to justify comparisons with Jesse Jackson. Despite the toppling of Saddam Hussein, a volatile world and delicate economy may ensure that the relatively unknown victor in the 2004 Democratic primaries faces a president about to follow in his father's footsteps.

Jimmy Carter was much derided during his term of office—especially toward the end when he appeared ineffectual in his response to the hostage crisis in Iran. After leaving the White House, however, Carter slowly established himself as a global ambassador, with a particular commitment to promoting Third World interests. In December 2002 he was awarded the Nobel Peace Prize a few months after he and Rosalyn spent six days in Cuba in an effort to improve relations between the U.S. and Fidel Castro's regime (left).

Editor's Note

The publication of this book has been a global effort, drawing on the expertise and knowledge of researchers and photographers within Getty Images as well as our partner agencies and many varied image sources. We at Getty Images are justly proud of our remarkable photographic collections. Our resources include Archive Photos in New York, which traces its lineage back to the oldest syndicated news agency in the United States, and FPG, whose stated aim was to champion the best in freelance photographers the United States had to offer.

In addition to Jennifer Jeffrey, who led all the picture research, we would like to thank Nicholas Webb and especially picture researcher Mitch Blank at Getty Images in New York for their knowledge and expertise. In addition, our partners Time Life, whose archive, founded on Henry Luce's internationally renowned *Life* magazine, was made accessible through the help of Jeff Burak at Time Inc. As always, the Getty Images team in London, both at Hulton Archive and Getty Images News & Sport, made the myriad collections at the archive accessible. Particular thanks go to Matthew Butson and Ali Khoja at Hulton Archive. The majority of the contemporary material is drawn from the rapidly expanding Getty Images News division.

Beyond the Getty Images family we offer our thanks to:
Ben Fathers at Agence France Presse, Piriya Vonghasemsiri at the Chicago Historical Society, Coi Drummond-Gehrig at the Western History/Genealogy Dept., Denver Public Library, Nancy Sherbert and Christie Stanley at Kansas State Historical Society, Kia Campbell and Bonnie Coles at the Library of Congress, Karen Anson at the Franklin D. Roosevelt Library, Jim Hill at the John Fitzgerald Kennedy Library, Philip Scott at the Lyndon Baines Johnson Library, Jessica Kratz at the Center for Legislative Archives, and Jim Parker at Double Delta Industries Inc., Tom Lisanti at the New York Public Library, Eleanor Gillers at the New York Historical Society, John Hallberg at the North Dakota State University Archives, Lillie Kerr at the Oklahoma Historical Society Archives, and Steven Williams at the Center for American History, University of Texas at Austin.

Master William J. Clinton of Hope, Arkansas, putting in early preparation for a long career in the limelight (left).

Alfred Eisenstaedt (following pages, top left) was born in Germany and emigrated to the U.S. in 1935, preceded by a fine reputation in European photojournalism. Along with Margaret Bourke-White, he was one of the original *Life* photographers and shot nearly one hundred covers for the magazine during its heyday. Great examples of his work can be seen on pages 186 and 261.

Carl Mydans (following pages, bottom left) covered both the European and Japanese theaters of World War II for *Life* and, with his reporter wife Shelley Smith, was imprisoned by the Japanese for two years. Mydans also covered the Korean War, where he took many memorable photographs of General MacArthur capturing this mercurial man's many moods (page 235 is a revealing example).

Life magazine photographer Margaret Bourke-White (following pages, right, with a Jesuit priest on assignment in 1953). Bourke-White was perhaps the most celebrated photojournalist of her era and one of the most famous of her photographs appears on pages 184–85.

Picture Acknowledgments

This book was produced by Getty Images Publishing Projects. We are grateful to the following sources for their kind assistance.

Agence France Presse Paul K. Buck 342t; **Chicago Historical Society**, Chicago Daily News [Neg.DN-0086586], 130t; **Denver Public Library**, Western History Collection [Rh-1334] Harry M. Rhoads 173t; **Duke University**, Rare Book, MS and Special Collections Library 82b; **Courtesy Lyndon Baines Johnson Library** Yoichi Okamoto 255, 287; **Kansas State Historical Society** 42-43; **Courtesy John Fitzgerald Kennedy Library** Cecil Stoughton/White House 274, Robert Knudsen/White House 275, Abbie Rowe/National Park Service 279; **Library of Congress** Prints and Photographs Division [LC-USZC4-4730] Ben Shahn 9b, [LC-USZ62-99664] 12, [LC-USZ62-1979] 16, [LC-USZ62-1562] 17t, [LC-USZC4-2398] 18t, [LC-USZC4-2677] 18b, [LC-USZC4-7421] 19b, Printed Ephemera Collection (Portfolio 192, Folder 12) 22b, [LC-USZC4-970 DLC] Robert Cruikshank 23t, [LCUSZC4-7731 DLC] Allyn Cox 23b, [LC-USZC4-6691] 24t, [LC-USZ62-29206] 24b, [LC-USZ62-1582] 25b, [LC-USZC4-03878] 26b, [LC-USZC4-2713] Thomas W. Strong 29b, Printed Ephemera Collection (Portfolio 22, Folder 12b) 30t, (Portfolio 86, Folder 2) 30b, Theatrical Poster Collection 32t, [LC-USZC4-5606] Joseph Ferdinand Keppler 50, [LC-USZ62-36676] 51b, [LC-DIG-CWPB-00848] Timothy O'Sullivan 60-61, Printed Ephemera Collection (Portfolio 205, Folder 27a) 67b, [LC-USZ62-12572 DLC] John J. Jarvis 72-73, [LC-USZ62-7618 DLC] 75, [LC-USZC4-5409] Joseph F. Keppler 86, [LC-USZ62-76210] 87t, [LC-USZC4-7890] J. S. Pughe 87b, [LC-USZ62-97992] Frances Benjamin Johnston 88t, [LC-USZ62-51821 DLC] 91, [LC-USZ62-75578] 92t, [LC-USZ62-79431] 94t, [acd 2a07675] Jerry Costello 95, [LC-USZC2-6272] 97, [LC-USZC4-3800] Leon Barritt 98b, [LC-USZ62-26149 DLC] 99t, [LC-USZ62-116377] 103, [LC-USZ62-131706 DLC] 104t, Printed Ephemera Collection (Portfolio 32 Folder 6d) 104b, [LC-USZ62-34095 DLC] 105b, [LC-USZ62-92924] 107r, [LC-USZ62-25338] 110t, [LC-USZ62-70382 DLC] 111t, [LC-USZ62-110995] 111bl, [LC-USZ62-40388] Frances Benjamin Johnston 114t, [LC-USZ62-84435] 115, [LC-USZ6-1820] 124t, [LC-USZ62-59680] 125, [LC-USZ62-61303] 127, [LC-USZ62-12142] 128, [LC-USZ62-96165] 130b, [LC-USZC4-1588 DLC] Albert M. Bender 157b, [LC-USZ62-123278] Acme 181t, [LC-USZC2-1180 DLC] Cleo Sara 182tr, [acd 2a10941] Leo Joseph Roche 205t, [LC-USZ62-32833 DLC] 215, [LC-USZC4-6613 James Montgomery Flagg 219b, [LC-USZ62-7449 DLC] 220-1, [LC-USZ62-93429] Acme 229t, LC-USZ62-126777] Acme 231, [LC-USZ62-128478] UPI 272b; **National Archives** [NWDNS-179-WP-984] 10t, [NWDNS-4-P-200] 90b, [NWDNS-200-HN-LA-1 Jacob Lawrence/Harmon Foundation] 93, [NWDNS-165-UM-21] 113t, [NWDNS-165-WW-600D(5)] 118, [NWDNS-111-SC-24644] 120, [NWDNS-165-WW-78A(2)] 123, [NWDNS-44-PA-2170] 149t, [NWDNS-142-H-83] 156t, [NWDNS-179-WP-936] 199b, [NRHS-21-DCHIHIHC-HC298-298REXHI14(1)] 206-207, [NWDNS-44-PA-1945] 208r, [NWDNS-44-PA-

1263] 212tl ; **New York Historical Society** Neg.PR-055-3-15, 44; J. S. Johnston Neg.72309, 71; **New York Public Library, Astor, Lenox and Tilden Foundations** [809569] 58b, George Hayward [809906] 26t, William H. Rau [800817] 101; **North Dakota State University** Institute of Regional Studies, Fargo, Fred Hultstrand History in Pictures Collection 48; **Oklahoma Historical Society** Archives and Manuscripts Division, [Photo No.10602] 76-77; **Courtesy Franklin D. Roosevelt Library** [71-63] 142, [63-111(1)] 143t, [65-694(2)] 149b, [74-20(269)] 150b, [54-499] 157t, [71-160] 160t, [83-37] 161, [48-22:3908(30)] 162, [53-227(1581)] 163t, [66-275(34)] 164t, [92-46] 167, [71-82] 169b, [64-141] 171tr, [78-19(4)] 179b, [53-227(1751)] 180l, [63-294] 181b, [67-49] 194, [47-96:1214] 195b, [53-227(2184)] 200t, [74-20(393)] 211t, [74-20(397)] 211b, [65-357(C)] 212b, [65-588(1)] 213, [56-480(1)] 225; **U. S. Senate Collection, Center for Legislative Archives/The Washington Post** reprinted with permission/Clifford K. Berryman 227b; **University of Texas at Austin** Center for American History, Robert Runyon Photograph Collection [No.02973] 129.

All other images in this book are from Getty Images collections, including the following, which have further attributions.

Agence France Presse 290t; **Alan Band Photo**s 307; **Blank Archives** 83b; **Consolidated News Pictures** 304, 309bl; **George Eastman House** George B. Atzerodt 59l; Lewis W. Hine 108b, 165; **Getty Images News and Sport** 9t, 356; Jim Bourg 340; Douglas Burrows 335; CNN 334t; Georges DeKeerle 321b, 354; Richard Ellis 13b; Porter Gifford 341b; Joebeanie.com 323b; Robert King 357b; Barbara Kinney/White House 350; Darren McCollester 352b; Douglas McFadd 358tr; Brad Markel 319; Joe Raedle 357t; Jorge Rey 360; Andrew Serban 359t; Jacob Silberberg 358bl; Brendan Smialowski 358tl; Billy Suratt 352m; Mike Theiler 359m; Washington Times/Ken Lambert 349t; Jamal A. Wilson 346t; Mark Wilson 323t, 347,349b,358br, 353; Alex Wong 359b; WTN Pictures 321t; **Library of Congress** 8, 10b, 14, 19t, 20t, 20b, 21t, 22t, 25t, 29t, 31, 35, 37t, 45b, 46b, 47, 51t, 54, 57, 58tl, 58tr, 59r, 64, 67t, 68, 70bl, 74, 78, 79, 82t, 89, 94b, 109, 113b, 119, 131, 132, 135, 148, 154t, 174b, 175, 176b, 179t, 180r, 182tl, 192b, 198t, 200b, 203, 224b, 262t, 277, 278b, 291, 300t, 309t, Matthew Brady 17b, 56; Willard Combes 174t; Bolte Gibson 141t; Dorothea Lange 210; Russell Lee 147t; J. Howard Miller 212tr; Ben Shahn 182br; Washington Post/Clifford K. Berryman 144t; **Museum of the City of New York** 70tr, 80, 102, Jacob Riis 81; **Reuters** G. Reed Schumann 342bl; **Time Life Pictures** 84-85, 92b,121t, 121b, 122, 146, 147b,168, 176t, 182bl, 204t, 208l, 214, 216, 217, 228, 230t, 364t; Terry Ashe 298b, 316, 318t, 318b, 333m, 341tl, 314tr, 342br, 344t, 344b; Bradford Bachrach 137; Lee Balterman 289, 298t, 299; Charles Bonnay 292t; Margaret Bourke-White 143b, 164b, 184-5, 365; Bill Bridges 245t; Dan Budnik/Woodfin Camp 283; Robert Burgess 324t; Larry Burrows 286; Tim Chapman 324b; Ed Clark 246;

Ralph Crane 248, 266t, Back cover; Don Cravens 242; Urbano Delvalle 322; Sahm Doherty 310r; John Dominis 1, 268; Alfred Eisenstaedt 171tl, 183tl, 186, 261; Thomas S. England 296; Bill Eppridge 266b, 293, 295b, 306t; Steven Frisch 290b; Bob Gomel 280; Allan Grant 238; Dirck Halstead 320, 328b, 343, 351, 352t; Rex Hardy Jr. 189; Bob Henriques 236b; Shel Hershorn 272t; Martha Holmes 233; Carl Iwasaki 328t; Yale Joel 232tl; Cynthia Johnson 314, 339, 348; Mark Kauffman 236t; Robert W. Kelley 271; James Keyser 337; Dorothea Lange 169m; Alan Levenson 334b; Steve Liss 330, 331, 336t; Thomas D. McAvoy 140t, 160b, 187b, 193l, 209, 245b; Leonard McCombe 232tr, 253t; David McGough 346b; Burton McNeely 273; Ben Martin 282b; Marvin Mattleson 326b; Michael Mauney 306b; Vernon Merritt III 11; Francis Miller 227t, 229b, 256t, 256b, 292b; Carl Mydans 235, 267, 278t; Steve Northup 303; John Olson 301; A. Y. Owen 243; Lynn Pelham 284; Hy Peskin 13t; Bill Pierce 259, 308, 333t; Art Rickerby 250, 276; Michael Rougier 239, 295t; David Rubinger 312; Mario Ruiz 332; David E. Scherman 140b, 187t, 190; Joseph Scherschel 260, 264b; William C. Shrout 222br; Paul Schutzer Front cover, 252, 253b, 262b, 264t; Art Shay 254t, 285; George Silk 364b; George Skadding 218, 234b; Eugene W. Smith 226; Richard Sobol; Howard Sochurek 6, 204b, 205b, 241, 281; Mike Stewart 363; John Storey 329; Allan Tannenbaum 336b; Donald Uhrbrock 265; William Vandivert 178tl, 178tr, 178b; Diana Walker 313, 317t, 325, 326t, 327, 333b, 345; Hank Walker 237, 244, 247,263; Julian Wasser 294.

For information about licensing Getty Images content, please contact your local Getty Images office.

Index

Abernathy, Ralph 289
Abzug, Bella 303
Acheson, Dean 201, 203–4, 230, 232
Adams, John Quincy 16–17
Addams, Jane 90, 111, 145
AFL-CIO 321, 329
Agnew, Spiro T. 301
Agricultural Adjustment Act (AAA) 142, 145, 155, 175
Albany Regency 17
Albright, Madeleine 320
American Expeditionary Force (AEF) 120
American Federation of Labor (AFL) 178, 238, 329
Americans for Democratic Action (ADA) 202
Anderson, Marian 144, 176, 339
Anthony, Susan B. 303
Apollo XI 301
Appalachian Development Act 257
Arafat, Yasser 350
Atlantic Charter 199

Bacall, Lauren 232
Bad Wound, Chief 140
Bank War 8, 17, 24–5
Baruch, Bernard 143
Bay of Pigs 252, 262
Begin, Menachem 313
Bell, John 21
Benton, Thomas Hart 183
Bentsen, Lloyd 317, 328, 331
Berryman, Clifford 144
Bethune, Mary MacLeod 145, 176
Biddle, Nicolas 17
Birmingham bombing 272
black cabinet 145, 176
Black Hawk War 18
Black Panther Party 291
Black Power 290–1
Blaine, James 48, 50
Blair, Francis Jr. 46–7
Bogart, Humphrey 232
Bonus March 94, 134
Booth, John Wilkes 59
Boulder Dam 144
Bourbon Democrats 52
Bourke-White, Margaret 184, 363

Boyd, Belle 58
Bradley, Bill 322
Brain Trust 143, 154
Brandeis, Louis 88, 107, 175
Breckinridge, John 21, 40
Brooks, Preston 20
Brown, H. Rap 291
Brown, John 34, 37
Bryan, William Jennings 9, 13, 53, 82–3, 86, 88–9, 96, 115, 173
Buchanan, James, 20–1, 37, 40, 72
Buchanan, Pat 11
Bumpers, Dale 259, 318
Bundy, McGeorge 252
Bush, George H.W. 11, 13, 317, 319–20, 331, 336, 350
Bush, George W. 11, 13, 16, 322–3, 352, 357, 359
Bush, Jeb 323

Calhoun, John C. 18, 31
Califano, Joseph 317
Camp David Peace Accords 259, 313, 350
Capone, Al 128, 158
Carmichael, Stokely 290–1
carpetbaggers 47
Carter, Jimmy 11, 50, 259, 310, 313, 316, 325, 333, 339, 361
Carter, Rosalyn 310, 325, 361
Castro, Fidel 252, 262, 361
Catt, Carrie Chapman 90, 111
Cermak, Anton 140
Chambers, Whittaker 203, 230
Chase, Salmon P. 47
Chavez, Cesar 329
Chicago riots 297
Chisholm, Shirley 258
Churchill, Winston 199, 201–2, 215, 221
Civilian Conservation Corps (CCC) 141–3, 145, 156–7
Civil Rights Act 1957 253
Civil Rights Act 1964 253–4, 303
Civil War 17, 44–6, 54, 57–8, 60, 62
Clark, James "Champ" 87–8
Clay, Henry 16, 31
Clayton Antitrust Act 89
Cleaver, Elridge 291
Clemenceau, Georges 91

Cleveland, Frances Folsom 13, 74
Cleveland, Grover 9, 50–3, 72, 74, 82, 316, 322
Clinton, Bill 8, 10–11, 13, 316–323, 336, 339, 341, 343, 345, 346, 349, 350, 352, 363
Clinton, Hillary Rodham 13, 318–9, 323, 336, 339, 341, 343, 346, 359
Committee on Civil Rights 227
Communist Party 146, 157, 184, 187, 204, 232
Compromise of 1850 19, 31
Congress of Industrial Organizations (CIO) 179, 238, 329
Connally, John 277
Connor, Eugene "Bull" 272
Conrad, Pete Jr. 300
Constitutional Union Party 21
Coolidge, Calvin 93
Cooper, Gordon 300
Copperheads 44, 58
Coughlin, Charles 146–7
Cox, Archibald 308
Crockett, Davy 19, 29
Cuban Missile Crisis 253–4, 266–7
Cuomo, Mario 316, 320, 333

Daley, Richard 205, 256–8, 297, 306
Davis, David 49
Davis, Jefferson 44, 54
Davis, John W. 93
Dean, Howard 323, 359
Debs, Eugene 92
Democratic Leadership Council (DLC) 12, 317–8, 336
Dewey, George 101
Dewey, Thomas 201, 203
Diem, Ngo Dinh 254
Dies, Martin 149, 187
Dixiecrats 10, 203, 229, 306
Dole, Bob 320–1, 345
Douglas, Stephen A. 20, 37, 40, 44
Douglass, Frederick 34
Du Bois, W. E. B. 203
Dukakis, Michael 317–8, 328, 331
Dust Bowl 166

Eagleton, Thomas 258
Eastland, James 205

Edwards, John 323, 359
Einstein, Albert 183
Eisenhower, Dwight D. 6, 202, 204–5, 236, 240, 242, 246, 252
Eisenstaedt, Alfred 363
Elizabeth, Queen 170
Ervin, Sam 308
Evans, Hiram 126

Fair Deal 202, 257
Farley, James 95, 140–1, 148, 193
Farmers' Alliance 78
Faubus, Orval 242
Federal Art Project 183
Federal Emergency Relief Administration (FERA) 141
Federal Housing Administration 145
Federal Reserve Act 88
Federal Theater 141, 149
Feinstein, Dianne 326
Ferguson, James E. 92–4
Ferguson, Miriam Amanda 93–4
Ferraro, Geraldine 316–7, 326
Fillmore, Millard 29
Fisk, Jim 47
Fitzgerald, John Francis "Honey" 87, 102
Flowers, Gennifer 320, 346
Foley, Thomas 320
Folk, Joseph W. 87
Ford, Gerald 309–10
Ford, Henry 148, 179
Frankfurter, Felix 203
Franklin, Aretha 339
freedmen 65, 67
Freedom Riders 253, 264
Freedom Summer 256
free silver 53, 82
Free-Soil Party 19, 20, 26, 40
Friedan, Betty 303
Fugitive Slave Law 19, 21, 31–2

Garfield, James, 49–50
Garner, John Nance 193
Garvey, Andrew J. 71
Geary, John 68
Gemini IV, V 300
General Agreement on Tariffs and Trade (GATT) 320
Gephardt, Richard 323, 341, 359

German-American Bund 188

George VI, King 170

Gingrich, Newt 321, 345

Goldwater, Barry 257, 280

Gore, Al 16, 49, 318, 322–3, 336, 352, 357, 359

Gore, Al Sr. 205

Gore, Tipper 336

Gould, Jay 47

Graham, Katharine 309

Granger laws 50–1, 78

Grant, Ulysses S. 47, 50

Great Depression 12, 94–5, 140–150, 154–6, 160, 166–9

Great Society 257

Greeley, Horace 47–8

greenbacks 45, 47

Green Party 322, 352

Guevara, Che 290

Guinier, Lani 319

Gulf of Tonkin Resolution 285

Hamer, Fannie Lou 256

Hancock, Winfield Scott 49

Hanna, Mark 53, 83

Harrison, Benjamin 51

Hart, Gary 317, 328

Hastie, William 145, 176

Hayes, Rutherford 49

Hayne, Robert 18

Health Maintenance Organizations 319

Hearst, William Randolph 86–7, 98–9

Hiroshima 202, 212, 216

Hiss, Alger 203, 230

Hoffman, Abbie 305

Hollywood Ten 232

Homestead Act 45, 78

Hoover, Herbert 93–5, 133–4, 136, 140, 152, 184

Hoovervilles 94

House, Edward 88, 90

House Un-American Activities Committee (HUAC) 149, 187, 203, 230, 232

Houston, Sam 19, 28

Howe, Julia Ward 37

Hughes, Charles Evans 90, 116, 152

Hull, Cordell 199

Humphrey, Hubert 4, 202, 205, 228, 245, 255–256, 280, 292, 298, 326

Hussein, King 350

Ickes, Harold 144–5, 154, 157, 174, 176

Immigration Acts 94, 257

Indian Removal Act 18

Interstate Commerce Commission (ICC) 51, 89, 253, 264

Iran hostage crisis 313, 325

Jackson, Andrew 8–9, 16–18, 22–5, 28–9, 32, 45,141

Jackson, Henry 308, 317

Jackson, Jesse 306, 317–8, 323, 329, 359

Jefferson, Thomas 8–10, 13, 50

Johnson, Andrew 44–7, 67

Johnson, Hugh 160

Johnson, Lady Bird 277–8, 285, 301

Johnson, Lynda 280

Johnson, Lyndon B. 4, 11, 141, 205, 240, 245, 252, 254–8, 260, 277–8, 282, 285, 287, 292, 301

Jones, Paula 320, 322, 346, 349

Jubilee Singers 68

Kansas-Nebraska Act 20, 37

Kaye, Danny 232

Kefauver, Estes 205, 240

Kennan, George F. 202–3

Kennedy, Caroline 252, 274, 278

Kennedy, Edward 259, 333

Kennedy, Ethel 294

Kennedy, Jacqueline 13, 252–3, 260, 274, 277–8

Kennedy, John F. 11, 13, 205, 240, 245–6, 248, 252–5, 260, 262, 266–8, 270, 274, 277–8, 300, 316, 331

Kennedy, John Jr. 274, 278

Kennedy, Joseph P. 94, 128, 142–3, 198, 260

Kennedy, Robert F. 246, 252–3, 256, 258, 264, 266–7, 292, 294, 298, 318

Kerry, John 323, 359

Khomeini, Ayatollah 313

Khrushchev, Nikita 252, 254, 262, 267

King, Coretta 246, 282

King, Martin Luther Jr. 11, 205, 242, 246, 253, 256, 258, 270, 282, 289–90, 294, 317–8

King, Rodney 318, 335

Know-Nothing (American) Party 20

Knox, Frank 149

Korean War 203–4, 232, 234

Ku Klux Klan 92–3, 126

Landon, Alfred 147

League of Nations 90–1, 122

Lease, Mary 51–2

Legal Tender Act 45

Lend-Lease 149, 198

Lewinsky, Monica 321–2, 349, 352

Lewis, John J. 147

Liberty League 147, 184

Lieberman, Joseph 323, 352, 359

Lincoln, Abraham 21, 32, 40, 44–6, 54, 57, 59, 67, 318

Little Rock demonstrations 242

Lloyd, Henry Demarest 53

Lodge, Henry Cabot 254

Long, Huey P. 146–7

Lovejoy, Elijah 32

Lowe, Seth 87

Lusitania 89, 115

MacArthur, Douglas 94, 134, 204, 234

McCarthy, Eugene 258, 292, 294

McCarthy, Joseph 203, 205, 232

McClellan, George B. 445, 57

McGovern, George 258, 306

McKinley, William 51, 53, 82–3, 86, 98, 116

McNamara, Robert 252–3

McVeigh, Timothy 320, 343

Maine, USS 86, 98

Manhattan Project 200

Manifest Destiny 13, 18, 19, 28

Marshall, George 224

Marshall, Thomas 91

Marshall Plan 202, 224

Meany, George 238

Medicare 256–7, 322, 352

Mercer, Lucy 145

Meredith, James 254

Mexican civil war 89, 112

Mexican War 19, 28–9, 112

Mills, Wilbur D. 256

Mississippi Freedom Democratic Party (MFDP) 256

Missouri Compromise 19–21, 31

Mondale, Walter 259, 310, 316–7, 326

Moon landing 301

Moorehead, Agnes 183

Morgan, J. Pierpoint 53, 107

Morris, Dick 318, 321

Moses, Bob 256

Moynihan, Daniel 319, 333

Mubarak, Habny 350

Murphy, Charles F. 87

Muskie, Edmund 298

Mydans, Carl 363

Nader, Ralph 322, 352

Nagasaki 202

Nast, Thomas 48, 70

National Association for the Advancement of Colored People (NAACP) 144, 176

National Labor Relations Board 147

National Recovery Administration (NRA) 142, 145, 147, 160, 175

National Youth Administration (NYA) 141, 145, 147

Neutrality Act 149, 191

New Deal 9–10 141–9, 155–6, 160–5, 173, 175, 183–4, 199, 200, 202, 205, 321

New Democrats 10–11

New Freedom 88, 107

New Nationalism 88

Newton, Huey 291

Nixon, Richard M. 203–5, 230, 234, 236, 246, 258, 298, 306, 308–9, 352

North American Free Trade Agreement (NAFTA) 320, 341

North Atlantic Treaty Organisation (NATO) 224

Noyes, Florence F. 110

Nunn, Sam 259, 317–9, 341

Nye Committee 149

Oklahoma bombing 320–1, 343

Olsen, Floyd 146

Oswald, Lee Harvey 254, 278

Palmer, A. Mitchell 92, 124
Panama Canal 86, 89
Peace Democrats 57, 60
Pearl Harbor 198–9, 207–211, 254
Pendleton, George 57
Pendergast, Jim and Tom 87
Perkins, Frances 94, 145–7, 154, 180–1
Perot, Ross 319
Pershing, John Joseph "Black Jack" 112, 120
Pierce, Franklin 19–20
Polk, James K. 18–19, 28
Pollock, Jackson 183
Populist (People's) Party 51–3, 78, 82, 86, 88
Potsdam Conference 201
Powell, Colin 319, 341
Progressive Citizens of America 202
Progressive Democrats 228
Prohibition 92, 94, 128, 158
Public Works Administration (PWA) 141, 144, 162, 183
Pulitzer, Joseph 86, 98–9

Quayle, Dan 331

Rabin, Yitzhak 350
Rainbow Coalition 12, 317, 329
Randolph, A. Philip 200
Rankin, Jeanette 198
Reagan, Nancy 325
Reagan, Ronald 13, 259, 325, 333, 352
Reconstruction 46–7, 49, 65, 67–8
Rector, Ricky Ray 318
Red Scare 92, 124, 203, 205, 232, 236
Reed, Stanley 203
Reno, Janet 319, 343
Resettlement Administration 143
Reuther, Walter 179, 238
Richards, Ann 320
Robeson, Paul 203–4, 232
Roosevelt, Eleanor 13, 136, 144–5, 170–1, 176, 200, 202, 219, 224
Roosevelt, Franklin Delano 4, 8–9,

12–13, 93–5, 130, 134–6,140–154, 157, 170, 173–6, 181, 184, 188–95, 198–201, 207–8, 211, 215–6, 219, 221, 223, 228, 248, 255, 316, 321, 333
Roosevelt, James 152
Roosevelt, Theodore 53, 86, 88–9, 101, 104, 116, 140, 157
Rosie the Riveter 200, 212
Ross, Nellie 93
Rural Electrification Administration 148
Russell, Richard 205, 255

Sadat, Anwar 313, 350
Santa Anna, Antonio L. de 28–9
Scott, Dred 20–1
Securities Exchange Commission (SEC) 143
Sedition Act 124
Seminole Wars 16–18, 165
September 11 323
Seymour, Horatio 46–7
Shahn, Ben 183
Sharpton, Al 323, 359
Shriver, Sargent 258
Sirhan, Sirhan 258
Silver Purchase Act 51
Sinatra, Frank 204
Sinclair, Upton 144, 146
Sister Souljah 318
slavery 8–9, 18–20, 29–37, 46, 58
Smith, Alfred E. 93–5, 130, 136, 145, 158, 205, 268
Smith, Ed 148
Social Security Act 13, 147–8, 180–1, 352
Spanish-American War 86, 98–101
Sparkman, John 236, 259
spoils system 17, 26
Sputnik 205, 300
Stalin, Joseph 199, 201–2, 215, 221
Stanton, Edwin 44, 67
Starr, Kenneth 321–2, 349
States' Rights Party 229
Steffen, Lincoln 87
Steinbeck, John 166
Stephens, Alexander 46
Stevenson, Adlai E. 6, 204–5, 230, 236, 240, 245, 252, 266

Stimson, Henry 149, 199
Stowe, Harriet Beecher 19, 32–33
Students for a Democratic Society 305
Students' Nonviolent Coordinating Committee (SNCC) 290
Strauss, Levi 39
Sumner, Charles 20
Sweeney, John 321–2
Symington, Stuart 205

Taft-Hartley Act 202, 227
Taft, William H. 88, 91, 104
Tammany Hall 12, 26, 48, 70–1, 87, 92, 94, 130, 145
Taney, Roger 20
Taylor, Zachary 29
Tehran Conference 215
Tennessee Valley Authority (TVA) 10, 143–5, 149, 164
Thurmond, Strom 227–9
Tilden, Samuel 48–9, 70
Tillman, Ben "Pitchfork" 53
Townsend, Charles 147
Tripp, Linda 322
Truman, Bess 223
Truman Doctrine 224
Truman, Harry S. 10, 200–4, 216, 219, 223–4, 227, 230, 234, 257
Truman, Margaret 223
Trumbo, Dalton 232
Truth, Sojourner 34
Tsongas, Paul 318, 336
Tubman, Harriet 34
Tugwell, Rexford 143, 157
Tweed, William "Boss" 12, 47–8, 70–1

Union of Auto Workers (UAW) 178–9
United Nations 201, 224, 266

Vallandigham, Clement 45–6
Van Buren, Martin 17, 19, 26
Versailles Treaty 90–1, 122, 148
Vietnam War 11, 254, 257–8, 285, 287, 289, 297
Villa, Pancho 90
Volstead Act 128
Voting Rights Act 256, 258, 282

Wagner, Robert 95, 147, 181
Walker, Jimmy 92, 193
Wallace, George 272, 306
Wallace, Henry 157, 193, 200, 202–4, 227
Wall Street Crash 94, 133
War Industries Board 90
Watergate scandal 308–10, 316
Watson, Tom 52–3
Watts riots 282
Weaver, Robert 145
Webster, Daniel 18–19, 31
Welles, Orson 141, 183
Whig Party 17, 19, 24, 29, 40
White, Byron 264
White, Ed 300
White, Walter 144, 176
Whitewater scandal 320, 322, 346
Willkie, Wendell 144, 149, 193, 198
Wilmot, David 19
Wilson, Edith 91
Wilson, Woodrow 7–8, 11, 13, 86, 88–91, 104, 107–8, 112, 116, 122, 124
Wobblies 91
Women's Peace Party 111
Wood, Fernando 58
Work Progress Administration (WPA) 183
World War I 11, 88–91, 115–6, 119–20, 122, 149
World War II 11, 149, 191, 198–202, 207–8, 215, 221
Wright, Fielding 229
Wright, Richard 183

Yalta Conference 201, 221
Yamamoto, Isoroku 208
yellow press 86–7, 99
Yeltsin, Boris 350
Young, Andrew 289

Zapata, Emiliano 112